Write Soon and Often

The Life of a Bomber Pilot Through His Letters Home

ANDY THOMSON

 FriesenPress

Suite 300 - 990 Fort St
Victoria, BC, V8V 3K2
Canada

www.friesenpress.com

Copyright © 2016 by Andy Thomson
First Edition — 2016

All rights reserved.

No part of this publication may be reproduced in any form, or by any means, electronic or mechanical, including photocopying, recording, or any information browsing, storage, or retrieval system, without permission in writing from FriesenPress.

ISBN
978-1-4602-9394-2 (Hardcover)
978-1-4602-9395-9 (Paperback)
978-1-4602-9396-6 (eBook)

1. BIOGRAPHY & AUTOBIOGRAPHY, MILITARY

Distributed to the trade by The Ingram Book Company

Table of Contents

Dedication v

Acknowledgements vii

Preface – Discovering an Uncle. xi

Prologue – Sunday, March 14, 1943 xix

Chapter 1 – Buggs – Growing up in Sudbury and Wye
(June 1, 1922 - September 1, 1937). 1

Chapter 2 – Porky – A Growing Curiosity about the World
(September 2, 1937 - May 21, 1941). 13

Chapter 3 – Enlisting: "The Proper Thing to Do"
(May 22 - September 2, 1941). 28

Chapter 4 – Learning to Fly
(September 3, 1941 - February 10, 1942) 40

Chapter 5 – Heading Overseas
(February 15 - May 5) 51

Chapter 6 – Adjusting to a New Way of Life
(May 1 - May 25, 1942). 69

Chapter 7 – A Soothing Cup of Tea
(May 26 - July 29, 1942) 83

Chapter 8 – A Return to Bonnie Scotland
(August 8 - October 21, 1942) 98

Chapter 9 – From a Crowd of Strangers to a Tight-Knit Crew
(August 15 - December 15) 111

Chapter 10 – Christmas Overseas
(December 15, 1942 - February 5, 1943) 133

Chapter 11 – Missions
(February 7 - March 12, 1943) 151

Chapter 12 – "Regret to Inform You…"
(March 14, 1943) 171

Chapter 13 – The Uncle I Came to Know 190

Appendix A – Chronology of Donald Plaunt's Life 206

Appendix B – List of Memorials Where Donald Plaunt's
Name is Listed 209

DEDICATION

To every parent and family member who received
those dreadful words: "Regret to Inform You…

To Donald's parents, Mildred and WB (Bill) Plaunt and siblings: Marion,
Kae, Bill, Helen and Jean, who lost their dearly beloved "Buggs"

To all those young men and women who answered the call to duty

ACKNOWLEDGEMENTS

A book like this does not get completed without the help of many people. First, my gratitude to my grandparents, who kept their son's letters, photographs, and most importantly, created a strong family legacy.

I was fortunate that my cousin, Sandra Kutchaw, gave me Donald's letters. Other cousins also contributed: Anne Benness, her mother Jean's photos, letters and diary; and Donald Plaunt, our uncle's pilot log book. I also got some great stories from Donald's sisters, Helen Vollans, Marion Mahaffy, Kae Thomson and Jean Benness, and his brother, Bill. My Aunt Agnes allowed me to search family records where I found mementos of Donald's life. My sisters, Judy Maki and Kathie Thomas, found me relevant stories and materials. I am grateful to my brother Robin for his ongoing interest and support in our quest to remember our uncle.

Through the internet, I met Alan Thepheads of London, UK, who not only found records of Donald's missions but sent them to me at his expense. Donald's close friend, Syd Smith, graciously permitted me to interview him and shared some of the materials that he published in his autobiography.

I benefitted from the instructive U of T summer writing course I took from Ken McGoogan, and for the feedback I received from the participants on my first attempts at this story. Ann Perry asked me the most challenging question of all: "How is this story going to be different from all other Second World War stories?" While searching for the answer, I reconnected with Suzette Blom, a colleague from the class, who spurred me on at a time when I was lagging.

Ridley Archivist, Paul Lewis, enabled my search in the Ridley Archives for materials related to Donald. As well, Brian Iggulden helped me contact several Ridley Old Boys who shared their stories of "Porky." Our National Archives provided Donald's military record. Jim Lutz contributed some excellent books on Bomber Command that were most helpful. Ron Foreman, my website manager, created a significant presence for the book on my website pogamasing.com.

Finally, I received valuable feedback from friends who read my first draft: Gale Jagoe, Richard Austin, Guy Mahaffy and Judy Lou Pugsley.

I had solid support from my family: Fraser, for feedback and suggestions, and Alex, for creatively organizing many chapters and editing the text. Mandy was my constant sounding board throughout, and also edited the manuscript.

My thanks to my Friesen's account manager, Judith Hewlett, for her guidance in publishing this story. Her thorough, congenial and timely responses to my questions made the publishing experience a positive one.

My sincere appreciation to everyone for your support.

See my website pogamasing.com for more photos and additional stories.

Photo Credits: Photos were from the albums of the Thomson and Plaunt families

THE PLAUNT FAMILY TREE DURING DONALD'S LIFETIME

The Plaunt Family Tree During Donald's Lifetime

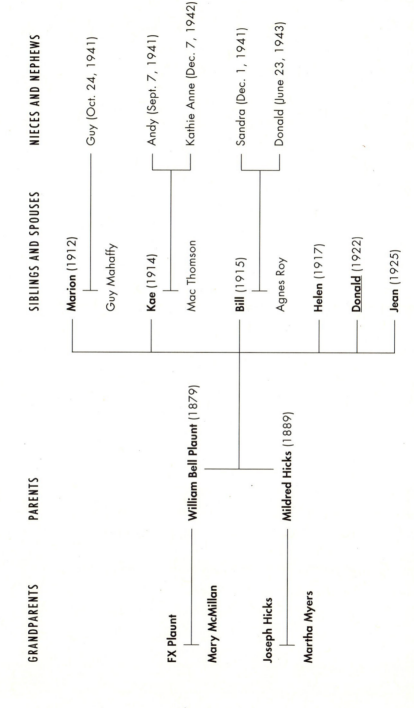

PREFACE
Discovering an Uncle

I knew I was destined to write this story after an incident on Parliament Hill in 1969. While a high school history teacher, I organized a student field trip to Ottawa to give my students an opportunity to visit our federal government and national museums. After attending a session of the House of Commons, we walked up to the Peace Tower, the iconic bell and clock edifice, which was built as a memorial to commemorate Canada's war dead. On the second floor, we found ourselves in the Memorial Chamber, which contains *The Books Of Remembrance*. The name of every soldier who perished fighting for Canada since Confederation is in one of the seven books. Every day at 11:00 am, the pages are turned, to reveal a new list of 90 or so names in each book.

I approached the Second World War Book, hoping to engage my students about the significance of the lists. As I got nearer to the book, I stopped abruptly. It was open on a page containing the names which started with the letter "P." "What a coincidence," I thought, but without a doubt, it ended there. I was wrong. As I looked closely, the name on the bottom right side of the page was too clear to deny. Of the 47,000 Canadians killed in the Second World War, that day the book was open on the page listing my mother's younger brother, WO II Donald Cameron Plaunt. After a few minutes, I regained my poise and shared this incredible coincidence with my students.

However, I wondered, if there was something more to this occurrence. Given that the book on the Second World War contained approximately 500 pages, it seemed more than just a fluke. As I thought about it, I remembered the other places I had seen my uncle's name memorialized which had little to do with fate. At Donald's high school, his name is etched in marble on The Memorial Wall at Ridley College with the eighty or so Ridleians who gave their lives in the Second World War. I also visited his grave in the Commonwealth Reichswald War Cemetery in Kleve, Germany in 1963. What I didn't know then, was that this twist of fate or "message" in the Peace Tower would be one of many I would come across on my journey to discover an uncle I never knew.

Formal Photo

Preface: Discovering an Uncle

At an early age, my uncle entered into my consciousness through two framed photographs in our Sudbury home. The first photograph was in a prominent place, so when I came in the front door, answered the telephone, or went upstairs, there it was. It was his prominent brushcut, about the same height as his forehead, that I noticed first, followed by his pleasant smile, and a pair of wings on his jacket. I knew little about him, only that my mother referred to him as "Uncle Donald."

A second photo on the fireplace mantle revealed a little more about him. Although he still wore a shirt and tie, his jacket was a khaki colour, and he wore a dark blue cap tilted to one side that covered his thick brushcut so prominently highlighted in the first photo. This print had been coloured to give him a more natural look than the faded black and white portrait near the stairs. But it wasn't the colour or the change in uniform that made this photograph more appealing. It was his beaming smile and friendly eyes. He appeared to be happy and easy-going, someone you could approach. However, since I had never known him, this person in the two pictures didn't have much importance to me as a young lad.

Mantle Photo

For years on Remembrance Day, Mother always placed a poppy on the wooden frame of his photograph. Once I was old enough to understand the significance of this annual tradition, I asked her about him. I learned that he was her younger brother and that he had been a pilot in the war. She also showed me a photograph of him holding a five-month-old baby on his lap on our front porch. It was me. He had been home on his last leave before he headed overseas. As it turned out, this was our only encounter. The image lingered.

In the main hallway of my elementary school, there were three large Group of Seven reproductions each dedicated to a former student who had lost his life in the war. One, *Northern River* by Tom Thomson, displayed the name "D. C. Plaunt" on a brass plaque attached to the frame. Now aware of the family connection, I often looked up to admire this picturesque scene and wondered what he was like, and why he died. But, he was still a mystery.

From family discussions and photographs I discovered that my uncle and I had some similar interests. We attended the same schools where we both played hockey and football; we had ventured to Europe in our youth, and both of us liked building model airplanes. Our strongest tie, however, was to our family. We shared a common family experience during the summer in a remote location near the CP railway line northwest of Sudbury. For Donald, it was with his parents and siblings in the village of Wye. For my family and me, it was with all my Plaunt grandparents, aunts, uncles and cousins at our camps on Lake Pogamasing (Pog), a few kilometres west of the same CP station. Donald's father had operated a lumber company in the area during the 1930's, and after the mill closed in 1940, he transformed a former logging camp on Pog into a family camp. My mother's tales of her family's summer holidays at Wye and their outings to the lake often highlighted my uncle's propensity for mischief and fun and gave me a better sense of his character.

But it was not from my parents that I learned about my uncle's role as a pilot. My mother's younger sister, Jean, married a former Air Force pilot, Barry Benness, who had also flown in the Second World War. While on occasional road trips with him to his pulp wood cutters, he entertained me with stories about his war experiences flying a Mosquito. Although he flew a different airplane from Uncle Donald's, he could answer my questions about the Lancaster bomber that my uncle had flown. He also talked about the number of his friends who never came home.

At 17, I went to Ridley College, the school my Uncle Donald had attended for four years of high school. There I met the headmaster, Dr. Hamilton, who gave me a warm welcome because he had known my

Preface: Discovering an Uncle

uncle. There had been a strong bond between them, and I began to form a picture of Donald that was different from the one presented by my family. I met many of his teachers: Mr. Morris, my history teacher, whom Donald had visited in England during the war, and Mr. Matheson, his hockey coach, and my Latin teacher. During Old Boy (alumni) weekends, my uncle's former schoolmates spoke fondly of his generous and fun-loving character.

When I graduated from Ridley in June 1960, I was the same age as my uncle when he joined the Air Force. I felt fortunate I didn't have to make the decision that Donald had made that year. Later in life, when my children reached that age, I developed a feeling of what it would have been like for my grandparents to say goodbye to their son. In his eagerness to enlist, Donald left Ridley the week after the annual cadet inspection in May, before the school year had finished.

After completing my last year of university, I travelled to Europe with three friends and a visit to my uncle's grave was included in our itinerary. He was buried in the Reichswald Forest War Cemetery, near Kleve, in north-west Germany, close to the Dutch border. As I entered the attractively manicured and solemn cemetery, I felt so overcome that I found it difficult to talk. After having heard so much

Donald's marker in The Reichswald War Cemetery

about him from my mother, aunts, uncle and grandparents, I was finally reuniting with him 21 years after he had held me as a five-month-old. Instead of being greeted by his cheerful personality, there was only a stone marker.

His grave lay with his six crew members in a row of common military headstones. As I scanned the cemetery I could see thousands of markers identical to my uncle's. No matter their rank or nationality, each had an identical stone with his personal information. What a colossal loss and a tsunami of grief those deaths must have caused their families. Shortly after my visit to the cemetery, I wrote my grandmother describing my visit. It was as if I had gone there with hopes that I would meet my uncle, and felt very let down when I didn't. For the first time, I felt a personal loss.

Later in London, I got together with my uncle's former rear gunner who was not on the plane that fateful night my uncle was killed. Jock Lochrie told me about my uncle's generosity, especially when Donald had asked his mother to send Christmas gifts for Jock's three-year-old daughter. He remembered Donald saying, "If I make it over my tenth mission I'll be all right." He made the tenth. It was on the eleventh that he was shot down. Like so many others who were not at their comrade's side when they died, Jock blamed himself for not being there on that fateful flight, somehow feeling that if he'd been there, things might have turned out differently.

Despite this early interest in my uncle, I didn't know how to learn more about his life and my interest in his story diminished. When I retired from teaching, I began to do some research and accumulated material on my uncle's missions and military record. But there was such a lack of information that I became discouraged. A fortunate break came one summer afternoon at our family camp on Lake Pogamasing. My cousin, Sandra Kutchaw, asked me if I was interested in a box of letters that were written by Uncle Donald. After my enthusiastic response, she handed me a golden Florentine box. I opened it to find a cherished cache of letters, telegrams and photographs. They had been saved by my grandparents and

Preface: Discovering an Uncle

were, along with their memories, the most precious keepsakes of their lost son. Another cousin, Anne Benness, lent me her mother's (Donald's youngest sister) box of letters which revealed a different side of Donald. Together they were a gateway into my uncle's character and his wartime experience. Finally, I had some substance to tell his story.

These letters revealed a young man who was describing the things that were most important to him: family, friends and his commitment to the war effort. At times, there was a tone of entitlement in his letters, but there was greater indication of a very caring, generous and fun-loving person. The letters began to fill in the gaps of what I had learned from people who had known him. While I hoped they would describe the military side of his life in the Air Force, unfortunately, any mention of combat news or his training was cut out by eagle-eyed censors. Fortunately, I met one of his closest friends, Syd Smith, who had enlisted and trained with Donald. Syd revealed much about their life in Sudbury and the Air Force.

Although the purpose of this book is to honour my uncle, I came to understand that, along with recognition for our war heroes, we should also recognize the important role their family and friends played. My uncle enjoyed writing letters with the expectation that responses would return quickly. His disappointment from the lack of letters, transformed to exhilaration and appreciation, when he received a bucket of them, especially after he returned from leave. Reading and writing letters was his way of coping with the incredible stress and homesickness he experienced. What better way to remove yourself from your present situation and imagine yourself with those you love.

The books I have read about Bomber Command are by men who survived their tour of duty[1], and later wrote memoires of their war experiences. Others endured time in a POW camp[2] or escaped through the

---

1 *A Thousand Shall Fall: The True Story of a Canadian Bomber in World War II.* Murray Peden. Toronto: Dundurn Press, 1979. *Boys, Bombs and Brussels Sprouts* by J. Douglas Harvey. Toronto: Goodread Biographies, 1983.

2 *Over The Wire* Andrew Carswell Mississauga, Ontario: John Wiley and Sons, 2011

xvii

underground back to Britain.[3] They are riveting and harrowing stories of what life was like for a bomber pilot who had the good fortune to return home. However, by the time these men recorded their stories, they were older and more mature. Given the high rate of casualties in Bomber Command (50%), thousands of young airmen never came home. Consequently, we rarely hear what the war was like for those who died. Fortunately, Donald's close friend, Syd Smith, wrote his autobiography, and I learned much from his story.

My conversations with Syd revealed an impression of my uncle as a cheerful, confident and extroverted personality. However, from Donald's letters, I detected a vulnerability that his comrades would not have easily noticed. From them, we get a glimpse of his thinking, illuminated by his use of the adolescent lingo of the day and his witty sense of humour. Fortunately, he was a prolific letter writer, and thus, I was able to build this compelling story.

---

3 *Lifting the Silence* by Sydney Smith and David Scott. Toronto: Dundurn Press, 2010

PROLOGUE

SUNDAY, MARCH 14, 1943

On a Sudbury Sunday morning, a family gathering was about to begin. The prolonged winter had made it difficult for families with small children to move about in the deep snow and sub-zero freezing temperatures. But with spring just around the corner, the matriarch decided it was time for a get-together to boost everyone's spirits. Soon after 11:30 am, the families of Mildred and WB (Bill) Plaunt began arriving at their home at 340 Laura Ave. For the grandparents, it was a joyous occasion. Nothing was more important than the gathering of their brood, especially when it included their four young grandchildren.

The Plaunt's oldest daughter Marion was the first to arrive with her husband Guy Mahaffy and their 17-month-old son. Her younger sister, Helen, met them at the door. She was living with her parents while she worked at the International Nickel office in Copper Cliff. Soon after, the older son, Bill Plaunt, WB's partner in his lumber business, arrived with his wife Agnes and their sixteen-month-old daughter. Agnes was expecting a second child in four months, so there was much excitement about the impending arrival. Last to arrive was their second oldest daughter Kae and her husband, Mac Thomson. But they had a reasonable excuse. With two young children, an 18-month-old son, and a 4-month-old daughter, punctuality wasn't as easy as it used to be. Two of WB and Mildred's children were absent: their youngest daughter Jean, who was in Toronto at school, and Donald, who was in Britain flying a Lancaster bomber with the Royal Air Force (RAF).

There was much commotion and excitement that enthusiastic youngsters can bring to a gathering. The three eldest grandchildren were playing with their entertaining and playful aunt, Helen, in the living room. She had a natural knack for engaging the kids so their parents had time to visit with the rest of the family.

Their father shared plans he had for their family camp on Lake Pogamasing. In the spring, he wanted to renovate the interior of the former cookery by building a fireplace and installing new siding and windows. Bill and his father talked about how the impending spring thaw would affect the hauling of logs to their recently constructed lumber mill at Raphoe, a small village on the CN line north-east of Sudbury.

Most importantly, all were interested in hearing who had received the latest letter from their 20-year-old brother who was now flying bombing missions to Europe. The amusing and upbeat tone of his letters diminished any concern they had for him. Their mother reported that Donald had spent his last leave in London with his two closest Sudbury friends, Bill Lane and Syd Smith. All appeared to be going well.

What turned an enjoyable family affair into a dreadful bolt from the blue was a quiet knock at the front door. Not everyone heard it, but Helen happened to be walking by, so she opened it to see a somber-looking young man. He asked if this was the residence of WB Plaunt. When she replied that it was, he handed her an envelope addressed to her father emboldened with CANADIAN NATIONAL TELEGRAM across the top. Receiving a telegram did not alarm Helen at first, as Donald had been sending telegrams regularly to inform his family that all was well. However, above the address was typed "REPORT DELIVERY," suggesting there was something different about this telegram. The courier politely asked Helen to sign the manifest and to give the telegram to Mr. Plaunt.

By now everyone realized something was amiss and they slowly gathered around their father. He opened the envelope and read it silently to himself; "Regret to inform you …" The instant change in their father's demeanour, along with his trembling hand that held the telegram, signaled that something serious had happened to Donald. Without finishing the complete text, he looked up and in a barely audible voice, told his family that Donald had been reported missing. After a few moments of ominous silence, Bill attempted to diffuse the tension in the room by referring to Donald's good friend Syd Smith, who was reported missing over France in December and was now back safely in England. This injection of optimism offered a sliver of hope, but in everyone's mind, there was a gloomy cloud of fear. How could their lovable and cheerful "Buggs" be a casualty of war?

It would be a painful period of several weeks before they learned the truth about Donald's missing status. Helen wrote to me many years later regarding that time: "I felt so alone and useless. The days following the arrival of the telegram was a very traumatic time for everyone, but endless grief for Mom and Dad." And even when his death was officially acknowledged, there existed a cloud of uncertainty about how he had died, and where his body was laid to rest.

For Donald's parents, the agony from his loss would continue to echo for the rest of their lives.

CHAPTER 1
Buggs — Growing up in Sudbury and Wye

(JUNE 1, 1922 - SEPTEMBER 1, 1937)

"Butter you, eat me Bug."

As a young boy, Donald possessed an irresistible charm and an entertaining sense of humour that made him the centre of his family. Whether it was fooling around in the high snow banks in winter, or playing games in the backyard in spring, he could always coax or charm one of them to join him. His slightly older sister, Helen, recounted one of those experiences when Donald was five years old.

Donald as a two-year-old

It was a warm sunny day in June, just after school had closed for the summer, and before the family headed to their summer home in a remote village north-west of Sudbury. Once outside, the two playmates headed for edge of the expansive back yard where their father had created a picturesque garden for his wife's enjoyment. The vibrant mixture of flowers and shrubs was interspaced among the outcrop of rocks, so prevalent in the hard-rock mining city.

1

The array of colour and scent was not only pleasing to the family but it also attracted a variety of birds and insects. While the two were playing a game, a passing butterfly caught Donald's attention. He instantly dropped the game and was off on a chase. Unable to trap the quick darting creature, Donald turned his attention to something slower and down to earth - a small brightly coloured insect. Helen noticed the sudden drop in excitement as he quietly stalked his new prey. He carefully cupped his pudgy hands around the crawling insect and after standing up, slowly opened up his palms to get a peek at his captured prize. Helen overheard him whisper, "Butter you, eat me bug." At first, these words were confusing and meant little to her, but it was one of those phrases uttered by a young child which captured the experience in his words. For Helen, it was the last word that resonated with her, and from it, she created the nickname "Buggs." Whether it was from what she heard at that moment, or for his persistent pestering at other times, the name captured the character of her younger brother. It caught on with the family too, and he became known by the new moniker. Donald must have liked it, because years later he signed a letter to his parents, "Love Buggs."

Every warrior's life begins in a family. For it is here that he gets his basic training: in self-reliance, relationships, responsibilities and values. He grew up in a loving and close-knit family which gave him the confidence and encouragement that nurtured him for what he became - a generous, fun-loving and mischievous character. Although his nickname was Buggs, he was more like a cuddly teddy bear.

Family Background

Donald Cameron Plaunt was the fifth child of Mildred and WB[4] (William Bell) Plaunt. He was born on June 1, 1922, in the town of

---

4   It was a Plaunt family tradition for males to be called by their initials rather than their given name. My grandfather was also call Bill, but mostly WB.

North Bay, Ontario, a railway centre and a mining and lumber town, on the north shore of Lake Nipissing. The family had moved there in 1920 from Renfrew in the Ottawa Valley so his father would be closer to his lumber businesses which necessitated regular travelling throughout Northern Ontario.

The Plaunts had met in Blind River in 1906, where WB had worked as a foreman for the Eddy Brothers in the booming lumber industry along the north shore of Georgian Bay. Mildred Hicks was teaching in a one-room schoolhouse in the small town of Thessalon, 80 kilometres west of Blind River. Although they became engaged in 1909, they decided to postpone their marriage until Mildred finished a nursing program. After she had completed her degree at Homewood, a psychiatric hospital in Guelph, the couple married in Sault Ste. Marie on March 8, 1912.

Mildred and WB had both inherited resilient family values from their parents. WB's parents, Mary McMillan and FX (Frances Xavier) Plaunt, farmed in eastern Ontario, alongside the colonization road west of Renfrew known as the Opeongo Trail. After he had finished his education (grade eight), WB worked on his father's farm in the summer months and logging operations in the winter.

One winter, WB and his father had to work in a logging camp to make some cash to pay off a friend's debt which FX had co-signed. In those days, your reputation was so important, that if you gave your word, usually on a handshake, you fulfilled your promise, no matter the cost. There was little cash in the economy as most goods were either self-made or exchanged by barter. However, this onerous experience for WB not only led to an opportunity to learn about logging, but it also spurred his interest in the industry as a career.

Mildred's parents were Joseph and Lydia Hicks. They had migrated from the United States in the late 1880's so that Joe could operate a saw mill in the Muskoka area. Joe Hicks was a short, stocky man who was a bit of a wanderer and jack-of-all-trades type, common in that era. As well as having been a mill operator in Muskoka, he was a driver of a horse-drawn streetcar in Toronto, a construction worker in Los Angeles, a police chief in Blind River, and ultimately, a carpenter and leather repairman in his son-in-law's lumber operation at Wye. Despite their nomadic lifestyle, the Hicks sustained a close family, bolstered by their deep-seated religious convictions.

The first home of newlyweds was in a logging camp near Mileage 71, on the CNR line north-east of Sudbury. When Mildred experienced complications during her first pregnancy, she had to move to Toronto where their first child, Marion, was born at the Salvation Army Hospital in December of 1912. After the birth, Mildred lived with her parents in Sturgeon Falls while WB continued to work in the remote logging operation. Dissatisfied by the separation from his family, WB found a management position in a munitions plant in Renfrew during the First World War. While they were living there, three more children were born: Kae, in 1914, Bill, in 1915 and Helen, in 1917.

After the war, WB returned to the lumber business and took a job with his Ottawa cousin, FX Plaunt, which precipitated a move to North Bay. A few years later, WB established a company with Ed White of Sudbury to cut pulp for the Spanish River Pulp and Paper Company at the source of the east branch of the Spanish River. Consequently, North Bay was no longer an ideal location as his work required him to be away for weeks at a time. In order to be closer to his family, they moved to Sudbury in the summer of 1924.

Their home, on the outskirts of the mining city, was a solitary house, a half a kilometre up a steep hill from the Canadian Pacific Railway station. The building of the CP transcontinental line in 1880's had become the focus for the development of Sudbury, especially when a blacksmith discovered copper and nickel during the construction of the railway. WB bought the house from a banker who had built his dream home on the outskirts of the city but unfortunately was never able to live in it.

WB (Bill) Plaunt

Chapter 1: Buggs – Growing up in Sudbury and Wye

The Plaunt home became the nucleus of a developing neighborhood and the centre of their family for decades. Within a few months of moving to Sudbury, a sixth child, Jean, was born in January of 1925. Despite the wide range of ages, the family developed as a loyal cohesive unit, creating a solid foundation which continued for generations.

WB and Mildred Plaunt were each solid characters and together, they were an ideal team. WB was a big man, measuring just over six feet tall and was as strong as an ox due to the tough, physical work he experienced on the farm and in the bush. Not only was he a hard worker, but he also had a natural affinity for the lumber business. According to his son Bill, who later became his business partner, he was a mathematical genius – a critical skill for estimating the value of timber limits. As a young teenager, Bill timber-cruised with him and realized that his father could multiply five and six-digit numbers in his head as fast as Bill could do it on paper, and do it just as accurately.

Mildred Plaunt

Plaunt was also a natural at dealing with people, as he possessed an inherent interest and concern for people who worked for him. He shared profits with the wood cutters and was generous to mill workers who couldn't afford to bring up their large families on the wages that some jobs paid. Every September, he cancelled the company store debts for the mill employees, so each started the next year with a clean sheet. He also provided a house for every family for a nominal monthly rent of $2 and medical care for his employees and their families for a dollar a month. As a result, the men who worked for him were exceptionally loyal.

Donald's mother, Mildred, had a gentle temperament that emanated from her warm appearance and confident personality. Her minister described her strengths in an application to the Guelph nursing program:

"I have found her to be a person of sterling character. She is worthy of all trust, bright, energetic and of a most amiable and willing disposition." Although she had personal ambitions, she chose to take on the traditional role of homemaker, as her husband was often away for weeks and the family needed a capable family manager.

WB liked to argue with his children to challenge their thinking. But he did not allow anyone in the family to challenge his wife's judgments. Mildred was always kind and considerate and treated all manner of people with equanimity. On many occasions during the Depression years, unemployed men showed up at their Sudbury home looking for a meal in exchange for work and she never turned one away. Together, WB and Mildred were a dedicated and compatible couple who provided a stable and caring home to Donald and his siblings. To each, the family was paramount, and each child was encouraged to become educated according to his or her interests and abilities.

Plaunt children in 1928, L to R - Donald, Bill, Helen, Kae, Jean and Marion

Early Years

Donald was two years old when the Plaunt family moved to Sudbury. Being the baby in a family gave him plenty of in-house attention. Along with a considerate brother and four caring sisters, he had a father who idolized children. WB did not have to travel for his business as much by the time Donald came along, and he was able to be at home with his family. He enjoyed Donald's enthusiasm and natural charm so much that he occasionally took him to work. There was no doubt his younger son was the apple of his eye.

For young Donald, the extra attention from his father was special, but it led to expectations of getting anything he wanted. In spite of Donald's position as his father's favourite, there was never any jealousy among the siblings as his natural boyish charm and entertaining humour dispelled that possibility. There was some rivalry, however, as his older sister, Helen, recounted; "Once I got over not being the baby of the family, we got along just fine." In fact, they were all often great playmates, as she and her sisters revelled in his fun-loving spirit. To Helen, "He was a cute little stinker with that curly blondish hair and those dimples, and with a unique nickname to boot."

Donald was a daredevil and loved to try things that he saw as the domain of adults. It was a way to show off his maturity, but it didn't always end well. One time, he borrowed his father's pipe and tried to smoke a mixture of dried crushed leaves. Unfortunately, he inhaled the fumes of this strange concoction, and he returned home feeling sick. His Grandmother Plaunt was the only one home and when she noticed he wasn't looking well, she asked him "What's the matter, Buggs?" He responded, "I'm not Buggs, I'm little Donald Plaunt, and I'm sick."

Sudbury Neighbourhood

Donald started school in 1928 at Central Public School, where the Sudbury Arena now stands, opposite the CP station at the bottom of O'Connor St. By 1930, his neighborhood had grown sufficiently, and a new elementary school was needed. As a result, Alexander Public School, was constructed on St. Brandon Street, no more than 100 meters from the Plaunt home on Laura Avenue. On the opening day of the new school, all the transferred students were to meet at Central Public and walk together to the new facility. Donald would have none of that. He wanted to be first to set his foot in the brand new school. So, as soon as he was out of his former school, he bolted for Alexander where Andy Grieve, the new principal, welcomed him as the first student.

Donald grew up in what was essentially a country home that slowly transformed into a neighbourhood as more families moved into the area. He developed friendships with a group of younger boys such as Tom Smith, Bill Reid and Bob Moss. Although they were younger by four or five years, it didn't matter to Donald. They played games together on the street or went hiking in the rocky hills near their homes. In winter, there were few organized activities, so they got together to play road hockey and build snow forts.

To Tom Smith, Donald was a "go-go kind of a guy" as he was always dreaming up fun activities to do with the gang. Because Donald was the oldest, he always told them what to do. But according to Tom, he was a decent boss, never ordering them around and always a fun kid. "What shocked me was what Don did with his model airplanes. He would build these model planes and take us up on the balcony overlooking the backyard of his parent's home. Then he would set his model plane on fire and send it off flying and crashing to the ground. I mean this was the Depression, and nobody would think of wasting money like that. This kid was just crazy."

Along with his passion for airplanes, Donald showed an early interest in the military. He joined the Boy Scouts at 11 and two years later, the Copper Cliff Highlander Cadet Corps. According to his brother Bill, he became a "professional Scot" and enjoyed both the military and Scottish nature of his cadet experience. In grade nine at Sudbury High School, he joined the cadet corps and played goal on the junior hockey team.

Although Donald had an anglicized French family name, he didn't like his connection with French Canadians. His Grandma Plaunt was a McMillan, and he preferred the association with her Scottish ethnicity. Helen remembered a French Canadian maid who loved to tease Donald about his name and who knew that the easiest way to get under his skin was to call him "Frenchy." Even as a young boy he would get upset with her teasing him and shout back, "I'm Scottish."

Donald in his Copper Cliff Highlander Cadet uniform

Wye and Pog

In 1929, WB Plaunt and his partner, Ed White, opened a sawmill operation to mill jack pine at Wye, a CPR stop, close-by the Spanish River and 90 kilometres north-west of Sudbury. The logs were driven down from the headwater of the east branch of the Spanish River to Wye, where alongside the river, they built a sawmill. This area of beautiful lakes and pine forests would become the home base for their lumber operation for the next decade and the future summer home for the family well into the next century.

Every summer, the Plaunt family loved to go to Wye, a miniature and rustic village that housed the mill workers and their families. The company constructed temporary homes with rough lumber covered by black felt paper. Civic services available in cities were unavailable in this remote village: wells provided water carried in pails, candlesticks or kerosene lamps gave light, root cellars or ice-boxes kept food preserved, residents used backhouses for toilet facilities and heat came from a wood stove. While the village looked gloomy, and the services were primitive, for Donald and his siblings, it was a magical place for fun and adventure.

During the summer months in this isolated setting, the six kids played and explored together as a family. Donald's older siblings, Marion, Kae, Bill and Helen were his first playmates until he met boys his age and could do things with them. There were lots of engaging activities for a youngster to do at Wye. The Plaunts had a tennis court behind their home; there were horses to ride; they could explore the logging roads and once or twice a day, they would cross the wooden bridge over the Spanish River and walk the sandy tote road to Lake Pogamasing for a swim. As in most small villages along the railway, the major event of the day was the arrival of the train. The CP train stopped twice a day for mail, express parcels or passengers. With the regular service, family and friends from Sudbury could come and go creating social activities for everyone. On the weekends when their father was present, they would head off to the lake for a picnic, usually to a sandy bay where a former logging camp still stood. Mildred called it *Billy's Bay* because her husband liked the place so much. WB had plans to convert his vacant logging building into a camp for his family once the mill was no longer operating.

As the Plaunt children moved into their mid-teens, the boys were employed in the sawmill while the girls worked in the office during the school vacation. Donald worked in the slab mill for a couple of summers while his older brother Bill took on a full-time job as the walking boss in the logging operation. By 1938, Bill had gained enough experience that his father made him a partner in the business and the company became known as W. B. Plaunt and Son.

Chapter 1: Buggs – Growing up in Sudbury and Wye

A Big Likable Kid

Along with the first group of neighborhood friends, Donald befriended a younger group of boys in his Sudbury neighbourhood. Donald's sister Marion remembered that he was wily at getting some of these kids to do his chores. When his father paid him to do a job, Donald, in turn, would hire the kids to do it for him. The group included Don Crang, and Ozzie and Jim Hinds. Jim remembered Donald hired them to wash his father's car and then he drove the gang to get ice cream or a drink at a local confectionary. He also remembered Donald's crazy driving; "He loved to try doing corners on two wheels" To Jim, he was a big, likable kid.

According to his brother Bill, Donald had a unique relationship with his father: "He could talk Dad into doing things that I couldn't get him to do. My dad had a lot of fun with Donald, and he was very fond of him. Donald had a great sense of humour and used to try to put things over on me. One time, Donald borrowed Dad's car, and cracked it up but didn't want Dad to find out. So he got it repaired and sent the bill to me." Bill also found him to be very stubborn. "He would do anything if you asked him to do it; but if you told him to do it, he just wouldn't do it, even if you tried to force him."

The Plaunt children attended boarding schools: the girls went to Branksome Hall in Toronto or the Convent in North Bay, and Bill went to St. Andrews in Aurora. St. Andrews would have been the preferred school for Donald, given his love of Scottish traditions. However, his brother got into some mischief and was asked not to come back for grade thirteen. As a result, Donald went to Ridley College in St. Catharines.

Donald's propensity for writing letters began at an early age. While his four older siblings were away at school, Donald wrote to them, as it was an era when people wrote to stay in touch. One of these letters he wrote to Helen, then in Toronto:

> I love you, I love you, I love you, but don't let that werry you.
> I had three mistakes in spelling bute don't let that weorry you ether.

I runded out of ink but don't lets that worry you nether.
Love Donald

His likability, sense of humour and dare devilishness would provide a sound foundation for his adolescent years.

The Plaunt family, circa 1935 - Front Row: Jean, Marion and Helen. Back Row: Kae, Donald and Bill

CHAPTER 2

Porky – A Growing Curiosity about the World

(SEPTEMBER 2, 1937 - MAY 21, 1941)

> At Ridley, he became known for three dominant characteristics; his size, his easy-going nature and his distinctive haircut. He also took on a new nickname, "Porky."

Off to Ridley

There is an expectation that when children go to boarding school, they will develop a degree of self-reliance, new interests and a broader perspective of the world. Donald's years at Ridley were this and more. Not only did he make friends with boys from other parts of the province, play a variety of sports and enrich his cadet experience, but he travelled to Europe on a school trip in 1939. Although I heard stories about Donald from many of his teachers and former friends, I wanted to gain some sense of his life at Ridley, so I wrote to a few of his classmates for their recollections.

Before Donald went to Ridley, he completed grade nine at Sudbury High School. He joined the cadet corps, played intramural football and goal for the junior hockey team. Donald arrived at Ridley in the fall of 1937 and quickly established a presence. He became known for three dominant characteristics: his size, his easy-going nature, and his distinctive haircut. He was also given a new nickname, "Porky," as he was a bit overweight. One former classmate didn't know whom I was talking about when I asked him about Donald Plaunt; however, when I mentioned "Porky," there was instant recognition. He was also known for his sweet tooth and his love of food which contributed to his chubby look. His height/weight stats – 5' 4 1/2" and 164 lbs. in a 1938 Ridley Physical Examination[5] - would lead one to describe him as being hefty, but not overweight.

Photos of Donald show him with the distinctive brush cut; it was thick, black and bristly, and it added about three inches to his height. Unfortunately, this hair style was unacceptable to Dr. Griffiths, the Ridley headmaster. Murray Snively, his nephew, and Porky's classmate, told me an amusing story about how Donald's haircut clashed with Dr. Griffith's perception of a proper Ridley haircut. He summoned Porky to his office for a talk and told him he looked like "a fuzzy bear." The headmaster ordered him to let his hair grow, with the expectation that it would slump over, and then it could be combed in an acceptable style.

Porky's attempt to tame his brush cut

Donald obeyed the headmaster, but his hair didn't. As Murray recalled to me, "Porky's hair continued to grow up and up." It wasn't as though he didn't try to manage his troublesome growth. In a picture of the Second Hockey Team, he had his hair combed down, or I should say, greased down. Regardless of the headmaster's orders, Porky's hair did not obey and consequently, forced the stern Dr. Griffith to capitulate. To

---

5 A year later he was 5'8" and 175 lbs. and in 1941 at his induction for the military 5' 11" and 190 lbs.

Chapter 2: Porky – A Growing Curiosity about the World

Dr. Griffith's credit, he called him in and admitted defeat, "Okay Porky, you win," Murray told me.

Even after sixty years, his Ridley peers remembered Porky's amiability and his sense of humour. Their words reinforced these characteristics: "a tough guy but lots of laughs," "everyone liked him," "he never offended anyone," and "he stood out."

The comments I found in the school's bi-annual journal, *Acta Ridleianna*, show Porky's development in his later years at Ridley. Comments about Porky did not appear in *Acta* until 1939, his third year. His large size led to the comment that he was "a human jelly roll that sometimes doesn't talk," to "laughter floats freely and frequently when Chester Lambert and his mates Buckingham, Plaunt, Franz and Pirie get together."

At the age of fifteen, Donald demonstrated his strength of character and commitment. His father was concerned about young people's consumption of alcohol and cigarettes so he enticed Donald to refrain from drinking and smoking. The deal - if Donald didn't drink or smoke until he was 21, he would earn a reward of $500. This amount doesn't sound like a large sum today but convert that value into today's dollars, and it would be considerably more. So it was a good deal if you had the willpower to abstain when most of your peers were drinking and smoking. Donald accepted the contract with enthusiasm.

A Trip to Europe - July/August 1939

A trip to Europe was a common experience for many young people of my generation when *Europe on $5.00 a Day* was a best seller. But for those who grew up in Canada during the 1930's, European travel was unknown. The motivation for taking the trip was a combination of interest in European history and English, his two favourite subjects, along with a personal connection to John Page, his housemaster, hockey coach and the trip organizer. I wonder how many other Canadian wartime pilots had the opportunity to have visited the places that they would later be flying over?

Donald's ship was to leave Montreal on July 7th. His parents turned the trip to Montreal into an opportunity to visit family members along the way. They stopped at Lake Clear where Donald acquired a pair of field glasses belonging to his late grandfather. Next, they stopped in Renfrew, the original home of the Plaunt clan dating back to the 1850's, where they met John McMillan, a distant cousin of WB's on his mother's side. In Ottawa, they had lunch with two Plaunt cousins, and then they motored to Montreal and checked into the famed Windsor Hotel. The following day was spent with friends seeing the sites of the city and the S.S. *Montclare*, Donald's ship for the Atlantic crossing.

The *Montclare* left Montreal the following day for the seven-day voyage to Greenock, Scotland. The journey down the St. Lawrence was quiet, although one of Donald's Ridley buddies, Bill Squire, got into trouble for hanging out of a porthole. Life on board their ship consisted of playing shuffleboard, ping-pong, tennis and darts, as well as walking around the main deck and socializing with other Canadians on student tours. There was some excitement along the St. Lawrence River as they ran into dense fog near Gaspé and had to stop until it cleared. Off the coast of Labrador, Donald, and his friends observed a close-up view of giant icebergs with his newly-acquired field glasses. Soon, rolling seas and sea-sickness curtailed the fun and games. Donald spent most of that day in bed but felt better by the next day. A bit presumptuous about his recovery, he climbed the crow's nest ladder, only to get sick again. He joined the group the next day for a farewell party in the lounge with a concert, singsong and dancing on the deck. Later that evening, the ship sailed up the Firth of Clyde and docked at the Scottish port of Greenock.

The Ridley tour was to travel through parts of Britain, Germany and France. Donald recorded detailed information about the notable historical personalities and events they encountered and places they visited. He was clearly engaged in the rich experience he witnessed as he wrote of his impressions in a journal and in letters to his parents. The history they

Chapter 2: Porky – A Growing Curiosity about the World

witnessed varied in time and place. However, there was one common theme in the streets - preparation for war.

Throughout the 1930's, global events were gradually ratcheting up to war; Japan had invaded Manchuria in 1931 and Italy followed suit in Ethiopia in 1935. The weak response from the League of Nations to these transgressions encouraged dictators like Adolph Hitler to flaunt the conditions of the Versailles Peace Treaty of 1919, and he began to rearm Germany. Furthermore, with no resolute response from the major powers to his illegal acts, the German chancellor sent German troops into the Rhineland (a de-militarized part of Germany) in 1936, and two years later, annexed Austria and took over Czechoslovakia in two stages. Then, in 1939, Hitler signed an alliance with the fascist Mussolini of Italy. As the dictator's rhetoric and threats of war escalated, European leaders preached appeasement. Only Winston Churchill warned of the inevitable consequence.

After the Nazi party came to power in Germany in 1933, they persecuted anyone who didn't fit Hitler's image of Aryan purity such as Gypsies, Jews and homosexuals. As well, political opponents, such as socialists, labour leaders and intellectuals, were interred in Dachau, one of the first concentration camps constructed to eliminate opposition to Hitler. The Nazi's committed atrocities, most blatantly on *Kristallnacht* in November of 1938, when Hitler's bully gangs killed hundreds of Jews. With little opposition at home and abroad, Hitler denounced the Non-Aggression Pact with Poland in April of 1939 and demanded the return of the free city of Danzig, taken from Germany in the WW I treaty.

Surprisingly, there appeared to be little concern from those heading to Europe that summer that the outbreak of war was possible. However, three days after the boat left Montreal, British Prime Minister Chamberlain responded to Hitler's threat, stating that Britain would guarantee Poland's independence. Finally, the British threw down the gauntlet; that meant, if Germany attacked Poland, Britain would declare war on Germany. France supported their British ally's decision. However, given the lack of resistance from the Western countries to date, no one took Chamberlain's threat seriously. Meanwhile, the Ridley trip carried on, and we get an eye-witness account from Donald's letters.

After disembarking near Glasgow, Scotland, two "wonderful old Rolls Royces" took them to catch a train for Loch Lomond where they boarded the *Princess Mae* for a trip around the famous lake. Donald observed that "The green water was very calm and the surroundings of chateau-like homes, huge mountains and trees, presented a very picturesque scene." Later on a bus trip, the driver pointed out the ruins of an old fort where James Wolfe, the British general who defeated Montcalm on the Plains of Abraham (near Quebec City), had been its commander. That evening Donald wrote in his diary: "The roads are very twisty and narrow and run in the valleys between the huge bens (mountains). When we neared Loch Katrine, we passed an old bagpiper who played for silver thrown from the bus. He was truly marvellous."

On Sunday, they did a walking tour of Edinburgh. Donald was impressed that the Royal Infirmary was "a free hospital, as are all in Scotland and are kept up entirely by voluntary contributions." After the 2,000-year-old Edinburgh Castle, they stopped at a war memorial that listed every Scot who fought in the Great War. He saw a monument to Ensign Ewart, the soldier who captured Napoleon's colours at the battle of Waterloo. As they walked along the main thoroughfare, called the Royal Mile, they walked through an alleyway that belonged to a man who led a double life that inspired Robert Louis Stevenson to write *Dr. Jekyll and Mr. Hyde*. Even as he was absorbing these noteworthy bits of history, Donald was keenly aware of the present. As he wrote to his parents on July 17:

> While we were in this town, a group of the territorial army went past mounted on motorcycles and a couple of army trucks passed us. There must be trouble somewhere as all the cities have hundreds of uniformed and armed soldiers in the streets. On Saturday we passed a whole column of army trucks, hauling men and guns. We saw

Chapter 2: Porky – A Growing Curiosity about the World

> hundreds of conscripts in Carlisle station transferred to an army camp. Also, on Saturday, a notice came out that no medical doctor may leave England or Scotland, or do so under penalty of the law. I saw a couple of bomb proof shelters yesterday for the first time, and it seems hard to believe I am in a land that must take such precautions as that ... I was talking to a Scottish boy around 14 years old, and he said everyone here has a gas mask.

After Edinburgh, they left for the Lake District of northern England. In Chester, a small town on the outskirts of Liverpool, he saw conscripts who looked "just awful." While most of the Ridley group hired a car to go into Liverpool, Donald, Bill Squire and Mr. Page rented bicycles and pedalled around the countryside and ventured 100 metres or so into Wales, "just enough to say we were there."

One extraordinary landmark that caught Donald's attention was Warwick Castle which had played a significant role in English history, especially during the War of the Roses. In his diary he noted:

> It is really a beautiful place; you walk in the entrance, which is a sunken road cut through the solid rock. A guide takes you around to the room displaying many kinds of weapons. Every type of arms imaginable hangs on the walls. From the hall, you go into the "music room" where there are all kinds of things including many suits of cap-a-pie (head to foot) armour, Oliver Cromwell's helmet, Queen Bess's saddle, many tapestries and fine pieces of furniture.

That evening they arrived in Stratford-on-Avon and attended a Shakespearian play. To his parents, he wrote that he "saw Shakespeare's birthplace among other things but what I enjoyed most was Warwick

Castle." In the face of all the significant cultural sites he observed, it was the military attractions that caught his eye.

The next morning they took the train to London and took a tour of the great historical sites including Buckingham Palace, Westminster Abbey and St. Paul's Cathedral. That afternoon, he had himself measured for a suit, telling his parents that he could not resist the bargain of $15 for a suit that cost $25 to $30 at home. That evening, they went for a walk around Trafalgar Square and Piccadilly Circus, the famous London landmarks he would become very familiar with when on leave from the RAF.

The following day they took a tour of Windsor Castle, and then on to Oxford, where they spent the rest of the day. Returning to London, they heard Paul Robeson, the famous American tenor and political activist, sing and they were so impressed with his performance that they stayed behind and got his autograph. The next morning they went to see the "Changing of the Guard" at Buckingham Palace and then to Whitehall to see the Horse Guards perform the same. Not wanting to miss a chance to see the prime minister, Donald hustled over to his residence at 10 Downing Street where he "roosted on a stone wall for 3 ½ hours" to catch a peek of Prime Minister Chamberlain. Unfortunately, he never showed.

Despite the daily excitement, Donald was frustrated that he had not received a letter from his parents and wrote to them; "I have received no word from you yet, but I am living in hope." But there was a more important motive for his letter. "I am sorry to have to ask for money, but I am very glad we are staying another five days." In a note to Donald's parents, John Page justified the rationale for staying longer; it was due to unsatisfactory accommodations on their return ship. He also added an observation: "Donald's questions show that he is taking a keen interest in all he sees ... His health has been of the best, which is reassuring, considering the changes in food, water, and sleeping conditions."

On their last day in London, Donald was cheered up by a letter from his mother. He went off to Canada House, the residence of the High Commissioner of Canada, and then for a visit to the House of Commons.

Chapter 2: Porky – A Growing Curiosity about the World

After an early dinner, they boarded the train to connect them to a channel boat to take them to the continent.

They travelled by train through Holland to Belgium for a stop at Waterloo, where, in 1815, the British and Prussian Armies, under the leadership of the Duke of Wellington, defeated Napoleon in the most famous battle of the 19th century: "Here I bought a sword for a souvenir. That night I went to a movie and after, we sat out in a sidewalk café and had a good time watching the people." He ended his letter with and all-too-common observation of his trip to date: "It is surprising just how Holland and Belgium are ready for war. Uniformed men everywhere."

Perceptions of Germany

On Saturday, July 29, they headed into Germany to Cologne, a city famous for its Gothic cathedral, and the forthcoming target of the "1,000 Bomber Raid" on May 30, 1942. They ran into a heat wave and a stubborn mother: "We had a reserved compartment on the train and out of the goodness of our hearts we allowed a woman with her baby to join us. The first thing she did was close the window so her child would not catch a cold and if we opened it the least little bit, she started shouting at us in German. So we left it shut and pretty near suffocated."

The uncomfortable train experience did not distort his view of the German people, as he wrote to his parents: "Well, here I am at last in notorious Germany, and the country is not half as bad as it is reputed to be. I must admit there are a lot of men in uniform hereabouts, but in talking to a couple of Germans, they thought there was little chance that there would be a war. As a matter of fact, the English are more sure of war than the Germans." As in the former countries, he noticed a variety of military uniforms. In Germany, he observed even more, due to the larger number of military and quasi-military organizations such as the Hitler Youth, the SS and the SA (two Nazi paramilitary groups). That night, they spent the evening walking along the Rhine watching the festive crowds.

The next morning, he recorded in his diary; "We had an uneventful trip up the Rhine to Bingham where we saw a recently burnt synagogue and a castle." In a letter to his parents from Heidelberg, Donald expanded on his observations:

> No one seems to think there will be a war. I asked one German, and he said England could not fight. I asked him why, and he said Britain has most of her army in Palestine. That goes to show you the propaganda that circulates here. Another told us that Canada would not help Britain and when we tried to tell him otherwise, he informed us we were wrong, and we know nothing about it.
>
> I was talking to quite a few German soldiers, and they are quite cheery chaps. Everybody here thinks the opposite to us. We believe it is Germany who is causing all the trouble, and they think Britain is the troublemaker and are going to start the war.
>
> It is apparent that the Germans love uniforms as I think every male in Germany has some uniform. They present a very smart appearance and look very smart. I believe Hitler is visiting a town not far from here tonight, and we all would like to see him, but it is impossible.
>
> Well, I guess I will close now and finish writing my diary. If I do not write you tomorrow, you will know the SS men have got me.

This last remark is the only hint that Donald was aware of the role of the secret police, but there is no mention of it in his diary. The only comment he made of atrocities committed against the Jews was the mention of the burnt synagogue. They spent another day in Germany, but this was the last entry in his diary. The trip continued to Paris, and then to London before they boarded the ship for Canada. However, we get a glimpse of his views of the French and Germans in his last letter:

> Well, now I am in 'Gai Paree' and it is quite a city. I haven't seen much of it, but this hotel is really elegant, it makes the Royal York look small time. It may seem funny, but I felt a lot better when I got into France from Germany. The first morning in Germany I sat down to breakfast expecting, of course, black coffee and black bread. My breakfast consisted of tea and <u>cream</u>, rolls, toast and <u>butter</u>, fried eggs fried in <u>butter</u> and a big slab of specialty back bacon, so you can figure out how disappointed I was. The thing I noted most around these countries is the men in uniform, thousands of them everywhere. I must say this for Germany. Her soldiers are in new, smart looking, well-pressed uniforms, while the French soldiers are dressed practically in rags. Most of their uniforms are faded, and the original colour scheme was a disappointed blue and others khaki.

Although there was no further record of his trip in his diary or from letters, it is remarkable that he was diligent at recording his observations of the trip for so long. His extensive journal and the recorded chats with people in the streets indicated his intense interest in what he witnessed. Clearly, this trip was a meaningful experience for Donald. His diary and letters revealed a curious seventeen-year-old who was maturing and developing a genuine interest in history and literature. His diary was jam-packed with much more interesting detail and insightful observations. The trip was also a test of his commitment to his father's challenge. While his buddies were drinking, Donald kept his word.

After he had returned to Sudbury in mid-August, he expressed definite opinions about the different nationalities he observed on his trip. Helen remembered he was "more British than the British when he came home." He was most impressed with the Germans and their "whistle clean" uniforms and their very disciplined behaviour. He didn't think much of the French, finding them to be an "untidy people." However, despite his more upbeat view of the Germans, he expressed relief once he re-entered France. He sensed something profound was brewing.

Two More Years of High School

Ridley College Cadet Corps - Donald before he became 2 IC, 2nd row, far left; Dr. Griffith, 1st row, 4th from left

By the time Donald returned to Ridley in the fall of 1939, the Germans had attacked Poland. The Ridley travel group had missed the opening of the war by two weeks. He was now in grade 12 and highly involved in the cadet corps, no doubt stimulated by his past summer experience. In the fall term, he played football, and in winter, hockey. The school journal reported that he was "the star goalie of the Seconds, and is pondering over the possibilities of medals and awards." He was also the captain of the hockey team that year, a rare honour for a goalie, and a recognition of his leadership.

In the 1940 summer edition of *Acta*, his house reporter described Donald as quite "spirited" and "When we step on the flat, we are immediately greeted by Plaunt's booming voice, either bellowing into the phone or settling the European question in no mean terms." Another reporter noted that Donald had given one of the two "most amusing speeches of the evening" at the dinner for the school soccer champions. The School House writer continued with another droll remark; "Donaldbain[6] Plaunt has put his sabre through comrade Watson."

Letters to his youngest sister Jean, who was a student at Branksome Hall in Toronto, provided an amusing insight into Donald's sense of humour. Since Donald was three years older, and in his graduating year of high school, he felt his big brotherly advice would cajole her into doing what he thought best. However, like her older sisters, Jean was no pushover, and she stood up to him, despite his condescending bravado. Regardless of his constant teasing, there was a strong affection between them. With her, he could act like a teenager, spouting off silly remarks but doing it mostly in jest.

His names for his sister included a basket of the teenage jargon of the day: Toots, Sugar Pill, Lizzie, String Bean and Lucky Witch. There were also amusing quotes. On her 16th birthday, he wrote: "A very Happy Birthday to you! Coming right along aren't you? Well now just imagine little Jean Plaunt all of sixteen years! Well, there is one happy thing, you certainly have them buffaloed on that ole adage, 'and never been kissed.' " He teased her about her dates and scolded her if she contemplated

---

6   Donaldbain was the second son of the murdered King Duncan in Shakespeare's *Macbeth*. Some mentioned Porky had a second nickname, "Dunc," possibly derived from King Duncan,. His sister, Jean, also used the name.

going out with a "UCC cad." Of course, he responded abruptly when any negative comment came from her: "Furthermore, watch your cracks about my beloved Ridley. You're looking for a 'fat eye' talking like that." And when his sister asked about a suspected girlfriend he replied: "Now my dear little sister, just what do you mean by that, how is Miss Smith, as wonderful as ever? I do not know who, or what you mean. Kindly explain yourself better in future." He admitted to her that he was writing babble. Before heading off to class he wrote, "I'll close for a while and finish shovelling later." After lunch, he ended the letter. "Well, Sweet Sixteen, be a good girl and if you find time, drop me a line, and if Father phones, remind him to write me. Be good and remember, if you cry on your birthday, you'll cry all year. Love, Donald PS WOW 8 PAGES!!!" He was pretty proud of himself, but it was an explicit suggestion to her to follow suit. "I don't appreciate a tiny 3-page letter after that super doozer eight-pager I tore off." It became a familiar refrain and not just to his little sister.

In his last year at Ridley (1940/41), Donald became a leader of the school, both as the adjutant and second-in-command (2IC) of the cadet corps, and a house prefect for School House, one of the four dorms. Although Donald made a name for himself in hockey, he also played football and cricket. One author described him as the "famous hoofer from Sudbury." He was a member of the First Football Team that won the Little Big Four championship[7] that fall.

His name occasionally appears in the game summaries of the First Team hockey games. The most notable being in a close game against Upper Canada where he "turned in a fine job kicking out plenty of labelled drives and proved himself to be a standout which helped them defeat their arch rivals." In the "Personnel" section of the First Team Hockey, the author emphasized Donald's positive attitude and consistent play: "With his great enthusiasm for the game, Porky was a source of inspiration and exhortation to all who came near his goal. He played consistently well all season, with some extra fine work in the clutches.

---

7   Ridley, Upper Canada, Trinity College Schools and St. Andrews

His forecast reads getting hotter all the time, but not much change in temperament."

Just the type of person who would make a capable leader in battle.

Porky as First Team goalie

CHAPTER 3

Enlisting: "The Proper Thing to Do"

(MAY 22 - SEPTEMBER 2, 1941)

"Oh, happy day! I've really got my fingers crossed hoping to be a pilot and I think there might be a fairly good chance."

Britain and France declared war on Germany two days after Germany invaded Poland on September 1, 1939. To demonstrate Canada's independence from Great Britain, Prime Minister Mackenzie King delayed the declaration of war by ten days. There may have been a hidden reason for the delay. Unlike the European countries that Donald had visited, Canada's Armed Forces were unready and ill-equipped for war. This unpreparedness was particularly true for the Air Force. There were only 270 aircraft and 3,000 personnel in the RCAF. There was much to do to catch up to an enemy which was far ahead in modern military aircraft and trained aircrew.

The expectation that young Canadians would enlist didn't materialize until Germany attacked Britain in August 1940. The daring heroics of the RAF pilots from the Commonwealth in the famed Battle of Britain resulted in an enthusiastic response by many young Canadians to enlist. No doubt there were other reasons for wanting to join: family military tradition, adventure, learning to fly and defending the Empire against the fascist dictatorship. Donald's interest in cadets and learning to fly made him an obvious candidate to join the Air Force. He also had a minor

Chapter 3: Enlisting: "The Proper Thing to Do"

trace of military tradition in the family as his Great Grandfather Myers on his mother's side had fought for the Union in the American Civil War. But when Donald signed his enlistment papers he recorded his only reason as "The proper thing to do."

The "Musketeers"

While in Sudbury for the Christmas break in 1940, Donald and his friends talked about signing up but postponed their decision until they finished the school year. In a letter to his sister Jean on January 12, 1941, Donald wrote; "Apparently our loving Father has given up writing, as I wrote him about the RCAF over a week ago and received no answer." I have no knowledge about my grandfather's attitude regarding Donald's enlistment, but like most parents, there would have been some reluctance. Young men think they'll never die; parents worry they will.

Donald planned to enlist with his two Sudbury friends, Billy Lane, a friend from Central Public and Syd Smith, whom he knew from the Copper Cliff Highlanders. All three attended Sudbury High School (SHS) and played on the same team in a six-man intramural football program. Their weekend social life at the YMCA extended this camaraderie where the director, Joe Barratt, organized Saturday night dances for Sudbury teenagers. They became close friends and Syd would often stay over at the Plaunt house after the dance, as he lived in Copper Cliff. Despite their different backgrounds - Syd's family had immigrated from England and his father worked as a shift superintendent at Inco - they became good friends. Sudbury's melting pot pooled kids from every economic and ethnic background. Syd described Donald as a: "big kid, but friendly and jovial, a bit domineering. But he knew his way around. Don didn't appear to be spoiled; he always shared what he had with us. He spent time with his folks. I can remember one night he had a group of us for a party, and I sat on the stairs and talked to Jean. In those days there was no drinking, it was just fun."

Three of the Four Musketeers: Mike Kennedy, Syd Smith and Donald

Although Donald was no longer attending SHS, he maintained his connection with the group of three friends whom Syd called "The Musketeers."[8] In the spring of 1941, they made their minds up to join up and during Donald's spring break they drove to the RCAF recruiting centre in North Bay. All three wanted to be pilots, Donald and Bill in fighters, while Syd preferred bombers. They completed their medical examinations that day, but they were told that pilots were no longer needed as the Battle of Britain was over. None of them was interested in being ground crew, so they postponed enlisting.

By May, the threat of German invasion had diminished because Britain's Fighter Command controlled the skies. As well, the RAF

---

8 There was a fourth member, Mike Kennedy, but he was rarely involved with them and didn't enlist until later.

bombers had destroyed the German barges that were to be used to ferry their troops across the English Channel for the invasion of Britain. As a result, Hitler focused on his next target, and in June, Germany invaded the Soviet Union.

Although the British controlled the English Channel with the Navy and the Air Force, there was a serious problem of shipping losses in the Atlantic inflicted by German U-boats. Consequently, Bomber Command stepped up its attacks on Atlantic ports to destroy German submarine bases and as well, laid sea mines to destroy enemy ships. Unfortunately, British casualties were high, and the German Luftwaffe demolished several RAF squadrons in these raids. The bomber losses were due to their inferior medium sized, two-engine aircraft that were overwhelmed by superior German opponents. As a result, Britain reinvented its bombing force by developing four-engine heavy bombers: the Stirling, the Halifax, and the Lancaster. This development was a turning point in the war and would make a major contribution to the eventual victory.

Given that the "best defence is an offence," Churchill considered the options that each of the three military services offered to provide an offensive strategy against Germany. Since the Navy was pre-occupied with protecting the Atlantic convoys and fighting the U-boat peril, and the Army was recovering from its decimation after its evacuation from Dunkirk during the fall of France, there was only the Air Force to provide the needed offense. So Churchill turned to Bomber Command to attack the German fortress. Bomber pilots and aircrew were now in demand.

Enlisting

The Sudbury boys learned that the Air Force was now recruiting. Bill and Syd headed back to North Bay to enroll, while Donald contacted the Hamilton RCAF office, as it was closer to St. Catharines. The day after the annual Ridley Cadet Corps inspection on May 21, 1941, Donald left his school to sign up. Because he departed so abruptly, his roommate, Hugh Watson, had to pack up Donald's belongings and ship his trunk home.

Among Donald's military records, there were three character references from Ridley. The Headmaster, Dr. Griffiths, wrote that Donald was "very keen, resourceful and enthusiastic ..." while Rev. Langhorn, the chaplain, commented that he "has revealed a cheerful personality, above average in principles with possibilities for leadership." The Cadet Corps instructor, Captain Iggulden, remarked: "I have no hesitation in stating that with a little more training, he would make a good officer. A trustworthy and reliable man." After an admission interview, the counsellor noted that he was "good fighting type - real pilot material," while another interviewer pointed out that Donald was "above average material."

There was also a self-assessment and interest questionnaire. For future employment, Donald indicated he wished to enter the military through Royal Military College and that he had prepared himself by completing seven years of cadet training: two with the Highlanders, one at SHS, and four at Ridley. He indicated that his favourite subjects were history, English and some maths. Academically, he placed himself 15th out of a class of 35, and 18th in mathematics. He indicated his preferred leisure activity was dancing, and he assessed himself as "average" in driving a car, swimming and riding. In answer to the "racial extraction of his parents," he replied "Scotch" which was a bit off, but indicated where his heart lay. His leadership positions included captain of the Seconds hockey team, house prefect, flight lieutenant and adjutant (2IC) of Ridley Cadet Corps and junior president of the Idylwylde Golf Club in Sudbury. When asked what aircrew duty he thought he could best perform he replied, "fighter pilot." The ten words he chose to describe himself (out of a list of 36) were: active, easy going, good natured, impulsive, like to lead and supervise others, persistent, restless, and self-confident. He stroked out impatient and lightly underscored lazy.

The British Commonwealth Air Training Program (BCATP) managed all Air Force training in Canada. Prime Minister Mackenzie King had advocated for the BCATP for Canada because it had the political benefit that only volunteers would be accepted. As a result, he did not have to worry about another political disaster, similar to what occurred in 1917, when the introduction of conscription tore the country apart. The goal of the BCATP was to train 30,000 air and ground crew annually. The air training program established over 200 training stations across Canada where they were safe from enemy attack and close to the United States, where equipment and volunteers could be acquired. Volunteers from other countries, both Commonwealth, and others were also welcome to volunteer. All Canadians trained in the program would integrate into the RAF until there were sufficient leadership and aircraft to form a Canadian Group.

At the enlistment centres, recruits signed all the official documents that contracted them to the RCAF. The BCATP would conduct preliminary training and assessment for all aircrew positions. Suitable pilot candidates would continue to flying school and, upon successful completion of two levels of flying instruction in Canada, proceed overseas for further training in Britain. At any stage of the training, a recruit could be removed from the pilot stream and be re-assigned to further training as navigator, gunner, wireless operator or bomb aimer. Most who enlisted hoped to become a pilot, but the majority were assigned to other roles.

The three Sudbury boys wanted to train together, but this didn't work out because they were called up at different times: Bill Lane first, then Donald, and shortly afterward, Syd Smith. After Donald had signed up in Hamilton, he travelled to the Manning Depot at the Canadian National Exhibition (CNE) grounds in Toronto. The CNE was a massive intake facility that could house thousands of new recruits. The new arrivals learned Air Force rules and expectations, participated in physical exercise for two hours a day, practiced military drills (marching, rifle, saluting) and, if necessary, could upgrade their academic skills. Given Donald's many years of cadet experience, this initiation would have been an easy transition. Assessing thousands of candidates took time, patience and an effective organization. While in this initial stage, duties and drills kept recruits busy for a few hours a day. Otherwise, it was unexciting, if not a boring, first few weeks.

After Donald arrived at the Manning Depot, he wrote to his father: "Well I am here at last ... there seems to be an awful lot of waiting around. They really treat you swell around here, not like the old army bull-dogging. The meals, so far, are swell, better than at Ridley. By bad luck, I am to be inoculated tomorrow and thus will be in sick-bay all weekend." The next day he told his mother and father: "Things haven't changed much since yesterday. A bunch of Englishmen arrived and are they ever enjoying the soft life around here. They are terrific fellows and are quite amusing. Saw Mr. Morris (teacher from Ridley) in fatigues dress and I couldn't help but laugh. Going to phone Bill Lane and hope to see him. I expect to be home on a 48-hour leave in a couple of weeks. Met some Old Boys from Ridley and some guys from Sudbury and aside from waiting, I am having the time of my life."

One of the themes in Donald's letters for the next few weeks had to do with his wants. He pressed his father for an automobile, as he was bored with all the free time and wanted the freedom that a car would provide. After a visit with a Ridley friend, Don Sorenson, he wrote to his mother, "I saw a swell car in Don's lot and thought I would like it, but Pappy sure put the jinx on that." A few days later he complained to her: "I guess I haven't the drag with Father that Willie (his brother) had when he was nineteen when he had a little Ford. Now I had a real good buy and offered to pay back most of it but, "no dice." His second priority was decent clothes, as Air Force issue didn't meet his standards. He asked his mother to buy "another summer uniform at Simpson's as they only give you one here, and you can't keep smart in that." After receiving a package of knitted articles from the IODE (Imperial Order of the Daughters of the Empire) he remarked: "I guess they realize I haven't a chance of getting any from home, being an uncle soon."

The possibility of training with one of his Sudbury pals happened when Syd Smith surprisingly arrived at the Manning Depot while Donald was in the hospital with pink-eye. Bill Lane had already advanced to the

Chapter 3: Enlisting: "The Proper Thing to Do"

Elementary Flying School, so there was little chance of a threesome. As Donald waited for the next phase, he boasted to his Dad of his future expectations. "Things are still very much to my liking here, but I am not a Colonel, or as the Air Force would call it, an Air Commodore yet, but give me time." Just before heading off to his next stage, Donald dropped another hint to his father about his most desperate desire. "That was a swell car I had lined up the other day. Just think you would have been paid back in two years." There was no immediate response from his father.

As often happened with military training, openings for the next stage of Don and Syd's instruction were full, so recruits were sent to an Air Force facility to mark time. The Ontario government had recently completed a new psychiatric hospital south of St. Thomas to house between 3-4,000 patients. Instead, it became one of the many technical training schools established to train ground crew and kitchen staff for the RCAF. Don and Syd were assigned to St. Thomas for a few weeks of guard duty.

The day before they arrived in St. Thomas, Germany invaded Russia, contravening a non-aggression pact Hitler had signed with Stalin in 1939. The Allies had gained another partner in their fight against Hitler. However, Hitler's attack on Russia wasn't as important to Donald as his father's acquiescence to his persistent appeals and Donald got his "swell car" to go to St. Thomas. In his letter of thanks, Donald described his Chevy sedan as: "a real smart outfit. It certainly is the berries. I got 23 M. to the gallon coming down, and there was no oil consumption. I had the day off yesterday so drove to Waterford to visit the Squires ... Will be home on July 12. Food not so good, warm weather kills the appetite. This place is too good for a barracks; some think it was to be a "nuthouse." I hope to bring home Crossie Clark on my next leave, if okay ... Don't worry I have never driven more carefully and I am not tearing madly around."

The only training Donald and Syd completed in St. Thomas was to learn Morse Code. Their guard duties were done in four-hour shifts, sitting in sentry boxes at the perimeter of the grounds, surrounded by a barbed wire fence. Daily afternoon parades broke the monotony that was intended to introduce the new recruits more to discipline than training. At this stage, his letters described what he did in his spare time - whom he was seeing, or his hopes for leave. He admonished his mother because he had not received a letter since June 19 (13 days prior), and Donald announced he was coming home on leave on July 19th. In case she missed that jab regarding her letter writing, he threw in another poke: "A fellow just came in here with two letters. I wonder what that feels like? Maybe someday I will know." He was thrilled to hear about the new boats for his family's camp on Lake Pogamasing (Pog). "I expect they are dandies." In a letter to youngest sister Jean, he wrote: "My little Chevy is just the thing down here. Boy, is it ever a swell little buggy." And after calling her a "Rat" for suggesting she hoped the Air Force would transfer him out west, he requested she "throw a little shindig, or if not, asked her if there will there be a dance at the Golf Club?"

Life at this post was monotonous, and his letters reflected it. He wanted to bring a girlfriend, Jeannie Ross, home although there was no indication if she ever made it to Sudbury. He was happy to learn that his mother had spent some time at *Journey's End*, her name for the renovated cookery on Pog, that was now the family camp. He was sheepish about letting his father know he was spending money, so he asked his mother if she could she lend him $10, but not tell his father. He had wanted to paint the side walls of his new "chariot." He used his new freedom to visit some Ridley friends at Lake Simcoe with Syd.

Chapter 3: Enlisting: "The Proper Thing to Do"

Donald with his Ridley friends and his Chevy sedan

Initial Training School

On July 28th, Syd and Donald moved back to Toronto to the Eglinton Hunt Club, newly converted into an RCAF training centre for the Initial Training School (ITS). This stage was most critical for those wanting to become pilots as its primary purpose was to divide the recruits into streams: pilots, navigators, wireless operators and gunners. There was intensive instruction in the theory of flight, meteorology, armaments, aircraft recognition, along with physical tests to see if the recruit's vision and balance were adequate to become a pilot. The hopeful pilots were evaluated in a flight simulator called a Link Trainer which tested an applicant's flying potential. Instructors were on the look-out for those with excellent math skills, the basis for navigators.

In a letter home, Donald mentioned that a fellow recruit from Sudbury lacked some basic toiletries and clothes, so he asked his mother if her IODE could send a package of these items to him. He also told her that he had taken his sister Jean out to the CNE, and spent a weekend at the Squire's cottage in Muskoka. He followed his news with an ever-growing list of requests. He asked her to send a decent photograph of herself; told her that he was going to write his father and "make a touch" for a good watch; and requested that she send his "silver-grey broadcloth shirt and towel fast."

The ITS course ended with an interview, followed by a parade, where the graduates, now known as Leading Aircraftman (LAC), were assigned to their next stage of training. All the recruits knew the location of the flight schools, so if you hoped to be a pilot, it was a crusher if you were transferred to a non-flying post. Donald expressed his hopes to his mother: "I hope as soon as in 2 ½ weeks I leave here, and I start my flying. Oh, happy day! I've really got my fingers crossed hoping to stay East and I think there might be a fairly good chance."

He and Syd got their wish, and they were posted to the Elementary Flying School in Goderich.

Before heading off to Goderich, Donald and Syd planned to spend their four-day leave in Sudbury to celebrate. Joyful at being selected for flight school, they were bound to have an enjoyable time and threw caution to the wind. First, they visited Donald's good friend Crossie Clark, who was recuperating from an operation in a Hamilton hospital. Then, they hit the road for Sudbury. Because there was no bypass around Toronto to the highways north, they drove through Toronto, the most direct route. His pledge to drive cautiously disregarded, Donald wasted no time getting to Sudbury. According to Syd, he was caught speeding three times through Toronto: on Lakeshore Road, University Avenue and Avenue Road, all three happening within a few minutes of each other. Back then, you could get a speeding ticket without being stopped by an officer, which was what happened to Donald. He didn't learn of his infractions for several months.

Leaving Toronto behind them, the exuberant recruits turned onto the Highway 11 northbound lanes. Halfway up the highway, Donald, distracted by his buoyant mood, realized he was running out of gas. With heavy restrictions on the purchase of gasoline, there were no places he could refuel. Dressed in his Air Force uniform, he wheeled into a police

Chapter 3: Enlisting: "The Proper Thing to Do"

station and asked for help. With the general support of the military high at the time, they gladly gave them the fuel to get home.

Just two months after his 19th birthday, Donald had all the dare necessary to fly, although he had yet to take off. All that mattered now was that he was going to Goderich for flying school. But first, Donald and Syd were off to Sudbury for a celebratory weekend at home.

CHAPTER 4

Learning to Fly

(SEPTEMBER 3, 1941 - FEBRUARY 10, 1942)

"If he flies a plane like he drives a car, he's lucky to be alive." *Bill Lane*

Elementary Flying School

This first stage of flight training in Goderich would include 150 hours of classroom and 50 hours of flying instruction, with a minimum of 25 hours solo. Service flying clubs across Canada operated the first level of flying schools for the BCATP. Since most of the instructors were former bush pilots, the atmosphere was more relaxed and less rigid than the disciplinary regime that Donald had experienced at the Manning Depot and ITS. In Goderich, they trained on the Fleet Finch, a fabric covered biplane, to learn the basics: taking off, landing, turning and climbing; and later, how to deal with stalls and fly with instruments. They received their first flying uniforms: a flying suit, leather helmet, parachute and aviator sunglasses.

Donald hit it off with his instructor, Jack Pequegnat, whom he described as "a marvellous flyer and a real good fellow." He was the brother of Doris Pequegnat, his sister Kae's close friend, from the University of Toronto Nursing School. In Donald's letter to his mother, he expressed his satisfaction: "Well, here I'm on a swell station. The country is flat and level for darn good flying. The food, the best yet, is catered by Murrays. The ground school work is more appealing than I expected. The only catch is that there is a lot of work and very little leave."

Chapter 4: *Learning to Fly*

Later he wrote to his father about his new base:

> There is practically no discipline, no "spit and polish" and a lot of work. We must study aero-engines, airframes, navigation, airmanship, signals and flying. We have 32 Fleet Finches for the 80 students on the station. The Fleet is the best training ship in Canada, and Goderich in one year of operation has had no accidents, so I guess I don't need to worry. The car is a blessing around here as we are 2 or 3 miles from Goderich, although there isn't much to do there. You find here that you're ready for bed at 9:00 pm. Syd Smith is still with me, so I still have someone here I know quite well. All the guys I did Guard Duty and ITS went to Windsor. Must go to the hangar. Oh yes, I am fairly flat and, as my raise hasn't come through yet, I would appreciate a slight remuneration.

A day later, Donald's mother wrote him to announce that his sister Kae had given birth to a son, Andy. Donald responded to her the next day on a broad range of topics:

> I received my "solo bracelet" that is my identification, and it is really swell. Thanks. I was in Toronto, and I took my kid sister out to dinner. She is certainly looking okay ... I was to Ridley during the weekend and saw some of the fellows. Not many of them are back. There is a surprising number in the Forces.
>
> The course here is quite stiff, and they weed you out quickly. Seven out of our original number of 21 have gone so far, and several more will likely be "washed-out" this week. It is no fault of the fellows at all. If you can't fly well and safely, away you go to Trenton and sit around

and maybe make an observer or air-gunner. So keep your fingers crossed for me on my 20-hour check. Jack Pequegnat, my instructor, told me to keep up and that I haven't too much to worry about. I soloed last week, and now have 3 hours solo and about 12 hours dual, so all the hard part is past. The rest is real hard application.

I am sorry to hear Grandfather (Hicks) isn't well and glad to hear Grandmother is up and feeling better. Give them my best. Re Helen - when does she go? So old "Drew" is quite the lad, eh? Too bad he is going to have brown eyes. All your descendants until now have had blue ones. I received a letter from Kae a while ago and for some strange reason, she seems quite proud of the little squirt. Strange, eh?

My Oxfords are wearing out and am in need of a new pair. Do you think I could get them at Simpsons? Also, did you say Pop was getting me a watch or no, because if he isn't, I will have to get one myself as my instructor told me I need one now? Let me know if you think he will, or I will get one on the old installment plan. Don't make it look like I am asking for it.

Well, Nanny Dear, I hope to see you in Toronto some weekend. Give my love to everyone.

To his father, on Sept. 25th, he added a few more details:

Nope, don't get worried, this isn't a touch. I thought it would be a nice change if I wrote you a letter that wasn't. Things are rather quiet here which makes it a darn good station for flying. By now I have approx. 20 hours flying

Chapter 4: Learning to Fly

time. I soloed at 8 hours and 15 minutes. This week I have a 20-hour check coming up. On that little trip I take the Commanding Officer for a ride, and if he thinks I catch on quick enough, I'm OK. If I don't, I am finished flying with the RCAF. However, my instructor and I both think I will likely survive.

The old rumours are floating around about our next station. It seems very likely that I will be going to Uplands Airport at Ottawa, which is a Service Fighters Training School with single engine Harvard airplanes. I had hoped to stay around here, but I did want fighters.

It is stormy here today, so we have to go to a flying school that isn't so popular. The senior flight moved out today, so I am a "Flight Senior" and now have a private room of my own – not much, but it gives a couple of nice privileges, like marching the boys around.

How was the trip up to Espanola with Parker and Miller? (his father's closest friends) When do you expect to be in Toronto? Maybe we can make a connection. I will be getting a 36-hour pass a week this coming Saturday. Best to all.

A week later he wrote to his father:

We get our wings at the next station (Brantford) and <u>then</u> we put in 50 hours flying time on the twin-engine Avro Anson. That means we will go to twin-engine fighters, which suits us fine. I had my first final exam today - wireless - and I think I did okay.

Thanks a million for the cheque for the watch. The one I have on order is a Rolex Oyster for $47.50 which is a real pip! My instructor is off sick, but not great flying weather.

Congratulations on winning the cup from Mr. Miller. Mom tells me it was a real tough match. No doubt Drew Thomson must be quite the chap by now. I would like to get home to see him and the new Thomson residence. I leave here in ten days, so I have a lot of work to do.

Donald and Syd with an Avro Anson at the Brantford Flying School
Donald, 2nd row, far left; Syd, 1st row, 3rd from left

Service Flying School

Both Syd and Donald headed to Brantford for their next stage of flying instruction. They flew an Avro Anson, which was formerly a twin-engine maritime reconnaissance aircraft. During this training period, the scope of the war had changed considerably. The Japanese had bombed Pearl Harbour on Dec. 7. The next day the United States declared war on Japan, and three days later, on Germany. To coordinate the Allied strategy, Churchill went to Washington to discuss the situation with Roosevelt. They agreed to focus first on the defeat of Germany. The best news received that day was that the Russians stopped the Germans at Moscow, giving the Allies hope that the Germans were not invincible.

In Brantford, their instructors were frustrated military pilots who preferred to be flying in Europe. "Well I am afraid I don't care for this station very much," he told his mother. "I don't like the food, the quarters, the airplanes and my instructor is a Frenchman – nothing like Pequegnat, shouting and cursing at me 2/3rds of the time. But other than that, I haven't much kick." A week later he complained to his father: "I can't say that ground school is going so smooth, you see, there is a lot of work, and it is quite difficult, and our instructors are not near as good as they were in Goderich. I guess that can be explained because this station is entirely government run."

However, things did improve as he told his mother: "Your letter kind of breaks up the pretty rigid routine around here. Incidentally, I am beginning to like it here much more than I did. However, ground school is demanding, but I think I shall be able to correct that with a bit of hard work." In a letter to his father, he told him: "Mother may have mentioned that my instructor, Pilot Officer Galen, is a Frenchman and I didn't like him. Well, after a while, I find that he isn't such a bad fellow. Well, I finally went solo on Nov. 5th in one of these big babies, and although I wanted single engines, it certainly is a great feeling flying a great big aircraft like this. I had no trouble at all – ready to go solo at 3 hours, but they kept me off until 5, just in case!" After telling his father there were lots of Brits, he joked: "Half the class with us are 'Limeys,' really not a bad bunch. So if I acquire an accent, you will know what has caused it all."

When not flying, recruits developed their flying skills on a flight simulator called a Link Trainer. "It's 8:00 pm and I am sitting in the Link Trainer room waiting to get a crack at it. It is darn tedious, and we have to put in 20 hours so it will improve our instrument flying." The following day he and his instructor crashed in a farmer's field between Cambridge and Paris. Both were shaken up, but it didn't appear there were any consequences as Donald was flying the next day with Galen. There was no report on the cause of the accident, although it was reported in the local newspaper. On hearing of the crash, Bill Lane commented; "If he flies a plane like he drives a car, he's lucky to be alive."

Donald's training expanded to include night flying, and longer day trips with a navigator. As he told his mother: "I enjoy night flying very much indeed. You have never seen anything quite so beautiful as the cities lit up at night from the air."

He kept in touch with sister Jean, hoping to coax her into setting him up with her friend: "Say, that _is_ a cute roommate you have. Too bad my _business_ prevents my looking into that matter a little more." After seeing a presentation at her school for the Crippled Kids (Sick Kids) Hospital, he wrote to her; "Here's one guy that kind of wished he had a peg leg and be entertained by some of that choice stuff I saw floating around there." He offered to let her use his car to visit her roommate in Oakville, along with some advice:

> Now I know how this "be careful" talk rolls off like water off a duck's back, but I think you would realize just what would happen to me if anything ever happened to the car, or especially you or your friends. My insurance does not cover any damage to my car. But if you bump into anyone and damage their car, don't be foolish and try to keep it quiet, let me know and maybe we can fix it up OK. I know all this pep talk about careful driving sounds foolish coming from me, but I also know the other side. But above all, have a great time and enjoy yourself as it is a month or so before you get home for Christmas.

He left the tank full and added, "This cash will not necessarily all go to gas, but don't get drunk on the rest!"

Donald was pleased to hear he was an uncle again, with two more additions to the family: a second nephew, Guy Mahaffy, and a niece, Sandra Plaunt. He asked his mother for gift suggestions, and he announced a pleasant surprise for his sister Helen. After he had departed for Europe, she was going to inherit his Chevy, as she needed a car to drive to Copper Cliff where she worked.

He spared no one from his constant demand for more letters. To Jeanie, he wrote sarcastically: "At last, I received that long-promised letter from you the other day. I sure was glad to hear from you after all these years." And to his mother: "I guess I will apply to some "Pen Pals" column in hopes of getting a letter from someone. However, this time, I shall forgive you again." He ended the letter: "Well, write soon and give me more dope. Make your next letter nice and long, and tell Dad he owes me one."

By early December, he was hoping to get leave for either New Year's or Christmas. He preferred New Year's, because his parents hosted a New Year's Day party that was a family favourite, as it included all their close friends, both young and old. Unfortunately, the Japanese attack on Pearl Harbour changed the Air Force leave program. He was very upset as he explained to his mother:

> Well, we have had a dirty trick played on us. We have no choice of what holiday we get. The whole station is being shut down for five days at Christmas – the one I didn't want. But here is what makes me so mad. The day we return, Dec. 29th, we begin our final exams. To top the whole thing off, there is considerable talk of the Christmas leave being cancelled altogether due to the developments in the East. That has happened in the Western Air Command, and there is the possibility it may occur here.

He received Christmas leave and after New Year's, he wrote to his parents: "I received the telegram from you, and it was very nice. I hope you had a good day "at home." Wish I could have been there, but swell during Christmas. Let me know what my bill was as I have to start on it sometime. My final exams start Monday, but I am afraid I am going to have quite a bit of trouble with them as I have never been too brainy as far as school was concerned. However, I think I shall scrape through … let's hear from you soon."

He remained in Brantford until he wrote his exams and completed his flying tests. His last flight was on January 16 before he headed to Sudbury for a five-day leave. Donald returned to Brantford for additional training and in the next two weeks added 30 hours to bring his total to 190 hours of flying. He was assessed as being "average" as a pupil pilot and navigator. His commanding officer commented that he "tends to be overconfident." Considering one-in-three recruits were "washed-out" from the start of the elementary flying school, being average was sufficient to advance. Both Donald and Syd received their wings after successfully completing their tests and exams. They had achieved their first major goal.

The other issue to be determined was whether they would graduate as pilot sergeants or pilot officers. To both Donald and Syd's disappointment, they graduated as the former, and so, were ranked as non-commissioned officers (NCO). Considering only one-third achieved the higher status (usually based on performance and marks) it wasn't to be expected. However, it was a letdown for Donald, although he admonished his mother for even bringing up the topic: "<u>Mother</u>, in your letter you talk of when I get my commission. Now listen, I wish you wouldn't talk about that as if it were a big thing. It may be to you, I am afraid, but to me, getting the wings is the big thing." Becoming an officer would have to wait until he merited it. Despite his protestations to the contrary, there was no denying; he craved it. After all, he had been second-in-command of the Ridley Cadet Corps and being an officer suited his self-image.

During his final two weeks in Brantford, he had time to play for the base unit hockey team and visit his grandparents. He found his Grandfather

Chapter 4: Learning to Fly

Hicks "looks the best he has been since arriving in Brantford." He told his parents he would be coming home on the 13th or 14th of February to say goodbye, as he was now bound for Britain.

Write Soon and Often

Graduates and Instructors of the Service Flying School at Brantford - Donald is in 1st row, far left, and Syd is 8th from left

CHAPTER 5
Heading Overseas
(FEBRUARY 15 - MAY 5)

"The Scotch people seemed real glad to see us and were all out having a great time waving."

Having passed the basic flying course for dual-engine aircraft in Canada, Donald was to head overseas for further training in two and four-engine bombers. It would be an unsettling time as he would be saying goodbye to his family, sailing across the Atlantic in U-boat infested waters and then settling into RAF protocol which would be more regimented than the RCAF culture he had experienced. It would also be an opportunity to live in a country that he had visited two years ago. But the young pilot had to keep another matter uppermost in his mind: he was going to war. Could the bravado of enlistment and the thrill of becoming a pilot maintain him in a distant land far away from those he loved?

Saying Goodbye

Sergeant Pilot Donald Plaunt saying goodbye to his sister Kae Thomson and five-month-old nephew Andy

Donald spent his five-day leave in Sudbury saying goodbye to friends and family. It would be a bittersweet time. His last trip home was an opportunity to become acquainted with a niece and two nephews who were born while he was he was training in southern Ontario. My father took our photo on the front steps of our family home with my rather imposing uncle and my mother. It captured my one enduring and endearing moment with him. His young friend, Jim Hinds, remembered Donald's farewell visit to his home to say goodbye and to give Jim his goalie pads. His mother had been a nurse in WW I and understood the grim consequences of optimistic boys who head off to battle. She was overcome by his parting visit as Donald had been a favourite. As he departed, Jim's mother wished him "goodbye and good luck," but there were a few tears after the door closed.

On Sunday, February 15, Syd and Donald and their families gathered at the CPR station in downtown Sudbury for the send-off. The eastbound troop train was picking up servicemen across Canada on their way to Halifax for embarkation to Britain. The Sudbury station was long overdue of a fresh coat of paint, and its dreary exterior set the tone for the unsettling departure of the troops. One can only imagine the profound anguish that their friends, family and especially parents, felt. For some, this would be their last contact with the husband, son or brother they loved. To conceal those disheartening feelings, everyone played an upbeat role, with smiles and cheers of "Good luck," and "Get back soon." Those leaving that day were keen young men, enthusiastic and ready to do their duty for their country. They were not feeling the forebodings of those they were leaving behind.

There was one ambiguous and disturbing story about my uncle's departure. Apparently, Donald told his brother Bill that he didn't think he would be returning. I didn't hear any details about the conversation, and unfortunately, I never had the opportunity to confirm the story with my Uncle Bill. I have read similar stories about airmen who felt a similar premonition, most notably in James Bradley's *Flyboys*, but I'm sure the feeling applied to many. If Donald did say this to his brother, his letters hardly showed any sense of this apprehension, nor did he ever mention it to his closest friend, Syd, who accompanied him to Britain. Donald's letters always portrayed a positive, upbeat attitude, and talk of his plans after his tour of duty. As a practicing Presbyterian, he believed that his fate was pre-determined, so there was no need to worry.

Donald described the train trip to Halifax to his parents: "We had a very nice trip down, and I received the best treatment I have yet received in the RCAF. We had a Pullman instead of the expected tourist car. The meals on the train were the very best too." The trip took two days, with stops at major cities along the way to pick up servicemen. There would be card games, story exchanges and much time to reflect. Of course, there would be much bluster and boasting of how once they got into battle they'd force the Nazis to turn and run. One could only imagine what they were thinking about once they were alone. It was a watershed moment; there was no going back.

Donald and Syd spent a month in Halifax before their departure. For the first time, the military censored Donald's letters. Donald was unable to tell his parents any military information, especially his embarkation date because he didn't know it. "Loose lips sink ships" was the adage that meant keeping vital military information secret, as there was always the possibility of a German informant in their midst.

Donald's letters revealed he was having a grand time in Halifax. He spent some time at the Nova Scotia Hotel, either writing letters in the Wings Club or attending dinner dances. He enjoyed going out for another reason. "Tonight I am going to a supper dance at the Nova Scotian. I have to get my civies out and have them pressed as I, a humble sergeant pilot, am not allowed to associate with officers and gentlemen. However, it is OK with me, as I am glad to get into a good fit again."

His spending habits drained his cash. "Okay, now, the explanation," he wrote to his father: " I wired for the cash for the good reason that I was very short of it. Don't think I have squandered all the money you gave me, but when I got to Halifax, I expected to be going right away and loaded up with a lot of articles and foodstuffs to take to people in England. Also, I bought a pair of boots. They cost $15 but are the real thing. Also, our pay hasn't come through to the station yet. Consequently, the wire you received also omitted to tell you that I lent money to a couple of the boys, and since the pay hasn't come through, they are, as yet, unable to repay me." In his next letter, he thanked his father and hoped that "the touch wasn't too much, but blame it on my expectation of leaving sooner."

Despite the grand time Donald enjoyed while in Halifax, he was also frustrated: "It certainly is an awful bind being kept on this station. There is very little to do but wait and let your flying become rusty." In the meantime, he was seeing some aircraft that tantalized him: "There are some superb airplanes around here in Halifax. All the real good ones you read about. I just can't wait to get my paws on a _real_ aircraft."

Donald received some sad news. His mother informed him that his Grandpa Hicks had died on March 1. Donald was concerned about his grandmother and asked if she would remain in Brampton. He asked his father how the Sudbury Victory Loan drive[9] had gone for the previous year as he had heard that the Canadian objective had been reached. He was eager to know how Helen was getting along with his Chev, "I think she should have a lot of fun with it." The mail that gave him the greatest laugh were the three speeding tickets he received for his trip through Toronto the previous summer. How it took so long to find him in Halifax is a mystery. But Donald knew what to do with them and promptly threw them into the nearest garbage can.

He spent some time with Andy Clark, the brother of his friend Crossie from Ridley. He met his parents' friend, Sub-Lieutenant Ian Collins, the only person that he bumped into one night from "back in Canada."[10] On March 11, he was at the Halifax Depot, ready for boarding. In a late night letter, he addressed a concern he knew would be uppermost in his parents' minds:

> This letter, I expect, will be the last note you will get from me. However, I will write a good long letter en route and will cable on arrival. I certainly hope you are not worrying at all. It is no strange coincidence that every troop ship has gotten across safely. Also, I am told there are 2 or 3 of Britain's biggest and best escorting us. The only thing I don't like is the fact that we will have to sit aboard ship in the harbour for about a week while the convoy is being made up and all that for five short days to cross.
>
> Well, thanks again and write soon and often to that overseas address. All My Love, Donald

---

9   His father was chair for Sudbury region.

10 Maritimers still thinking in pre-Confederation terms, sometimes refer to Ontario and Quebec as Canada.

"Write soon and often" would become a familiar refrain.

Despite Donald's reassurances, there was much to concern his parents about the Atlantic trip. Now that the Americans were at war, the Germans expanded their U-boat campaign along the US coast, bringing more submarines into the North Atlantic convoy routes. The shipping losses were horrific. The Allies suffered their greatest losses in 1942, with over 1,300 ships lost compared to 500 in 1941.[11] Most of the losses came from merchant ships that were slower than the convoy, as they were easy pickings for night time attacks when the U-boats could surface and attack the lone stragglers. No wonder they were called "wolf packs."

Bomber Command

As mentioned in a previous chapter, Bomber Command was also going through a major crisis. Unknown to Donald and Syd, Bomber Command had reached a critical juncture due to its abysmal failure concerning aircraft losses, and its inability to hit targets on bombing missions. The operational focus had slowly shifted from bombing precise military targets such as synthetic oil production facilities, U-boat ports - which were difficult to locate and strike, to hitting larger targets such as war industries within cities. As well, the bombing missions were shifted to nighttime to reduce the higher daytime losses.

These declining results convinced Churchill that a drastic change was required. He assigned David Butt, an assistant to Churchill's Chief Scientific Advisor, to investigate the problem and report his findings. The Butt Report of August 1941, clearly defined the problem: only one-in-four bombers were within five miles of the target on moonlit nights and one-in-fifteen on darker nights. Even the Germans were confused, as bombing patterns were so scattered they couldn't figure out what the

---

11 http://www.uboat.net/allies/merchants/losses_year.html

target had been. Consequently, Churchill ordered the reduction of the number of operations for three months to find a solution.

Critics thought Bomber Command should not take on the major offensive role against the Germans. Valuable resources were required elsewhere, such as in the Middle and the Far East. The Royal Navy complained the loudest, as they needed airplanes for Coastal Command to protect the Atlantic convoys. On the other hand, proponents of strategic bombing felt that it was the only option to generate an offensive against Germany. Also, there was pressure from Stalin to initiate a second front to necessitate the German military to reduce their forces from the eastern front to defend their western borders.

In February 1942, the War Cabinet directed that the new strategic focus of Bomber Command was to be "on the morale of the enemy civil population, and in particular, the industrial workers." Cities with major war industries and populations were now the primary targets. Along with the new policy, came a new leader, Arthur Harris, who vowed to pursue this aggressive strategy, despite its focus on civilians.

As Donald headed to Britain in March 1942, most aircraft in Bomber Command were two-engine bombers with a limited range and payload. Newly developed four-engine bombers such as the Halifax, Stirling and Lancaster would upgrade the capacity of Bomber Command. But there were too few of them. In a report to the War Ministry on March 1, 1942, there were only 62 four-engine bombers (only four were Lancasters) out of a total of 469 two-engine nighttime bombers and 78 two-engine daytime bombers. New navigation equipment and training bases, along with a substantial conversion of aircrew to the new bombers would also be required. It would be an incredible challenge to develop and manufacture the new heavy bombers. Britain's survival depended on this massive overhaul. Unbeknownst to Syd and Donald, they were on the cusp of these innovations. But would they be flying the older, ineffective two-engine bombers or the newer upgraded four-engine planes?

While crossing the Atlantic, Donald had time to write: "I am on a pretty good boat, and I am in a first class cabin with Syd. It was roomy enough that we let another fellow sleep under our bed on the floor as he had pretty bad quarters (most non-commissioned officers were in a hammock below decks). We're well looked after and have aircraft patrolling overhead. Apparently, a sub was moving in, and a destroyer went to town with depth charges and might have nabbed him." The food was: "fair and much better that I could expect ... There is not much to do but sit around and take life easy, with just an hour or so of boat drill every morning. Your field glasses are just the thing for peeking around the other ships in the convoy. I will be able to tell you more in a couple of months." He told his father about being interviewed by a Canadian Press reporter in Halifax with the hopes that his parents would see the article in the newspaper and learn of his safe arrival. However, the information in the article turned out very differently from what Donald had planned.

Bournemouth

After disembarking, and a seven-hour train ride from Glasgow to Bournemouth on Britain's southern coast, Donald sent a telegram.

> Telegram March 28 MR AND MRS WB PLAUNT CONGRATULATIONS ON ANNIVERSARY LOVE DONALD PLAUNT

The message of his safe arrival trumped his good wishes for their 30th wedding anniversary. The following day he continued the letter to his parents that he had started on the ship:

> Well, the story. I sailed from Halifax on March 14th and had a good trip across on the *Orbita*, built just before WW I. We had a very smooth crossing, and I didn't get seasick. The crew said the weather was exceptionally fine

for that time of year. It was a smoother passage than my other one in 1939. As far as Jerry went, he made a couple of passes at us, and it cost him two subs to none of our convoy. It was only a two-ship convoy, but we had two Yank destroyers who did a marvelous job.

We landed at practically the same place I did before in Scotland. The Scotch people seemed real glad to see us and were all out having a great time waving. We boarded the train from the boat and swooped away right down here to the south of England, at the world's most famous summer resort. The English were, of course, much more reserved but are nice just the same. As a matter of fact, one Englishwoman's kindness caused me great embarrassment. Another Canadian fellow and I were sitting in a restaurant having our afternoon tea and the waitress came over and told us that the lady across the aisle wanted to foot the bill. Well, I don't object to other people footing the bill, but this seemed rather different. Then, to make matters a lot worse, she came over and gave us a great pep talk of how our presence was appreciated and that England was in debt to Canada and all that stuff. Boy, were we glad to get out of that! However, that shows you just how the people over here felt.

We are billeted in the once swank Bath Hill Court Apt. Hotel in Bournemouth. It is a lovely building with our room opening onto a balcony with a marvelous view. However, we will not be staying here long. In two or three days I expect to go on leave for a week. What makes me mad is we have hurried away from home without much leave and then come over here and get 7-10 days, and then come back and sit around for perhaps a month or two. So far life around here has been _too_ relaxed. I can expect very little action until July or August, so I am not too happy about that.

As for the food in England, I received an awful shock. Happily, it was a pleasant shock. The food is better than Canadian Air Force food. Ice cream, after a fashion, can be bought and so can other foodstuffs in the restaurants. However, it isn't us that gets hit, but the unfortunate "Civie," and he barely gets enough to survive on.

The weather up until today has been marvelous, sunny, bright and warm, like April or May at home. We dumped our great coats the day we arrived. However, today we are enjoying one of England's famous fogs.

There is quite a bit for us to do re amusement. They seemed to be having a dance all day around here. Lots of plays and shows and the like. It is 10:30 pm and everything is closed, but to me, it seems like 2 or 3 o'clock. The black-out is not as bad as one would expect. However, they don't fool with it. They are on the lookout all the time. So far, I have heard the air-raid warning twice, but Jerry was only passing overhead. The people ignore him and carry on just the same. I guess it is because Bournemouth is about the least bombed spot in England. So, you can see, for the next couple of months, I will be leading a life of definite ease.

My clothes are all intact, except I find I need a new pair of slippers, size 10. You will have to send them as that sort of thing cannot be bought in this country.

Chapter 5: Heading Overseas

Well, I have talked about me and my experiences long enough. Of course, I hope both of you are in A-1 shape and enjoying life. Also, I trust that all the sons and daughters are intact as well. Be sure to give them all my best and tell them to write if possible. But the mighty mites! How are Drew, Guy and Sandra? I bet there is no holding them now, a real three-ring circus.

He ended to get the letter to his courier who was returning to Canada: "Don't think that I don't like lots of mail, so write often and give me all the dope. Be good and look after yourselves. All My Love, Donald"

There was no doubt in Donald's mind that the distance between him and his family was now greater than the ocean he had just crossed. His expectation would be to hear from them often, to reduce that gap and to sustain his morale. As his training progressed, each letter or telegram sent home would confirm something more important than the content - he was alive. However, no matter how regularly both Donald and his family tried to write, delays for a multitude of reasons interrupted the flow of letters, causing much anguish on both sides of the Atlantic.

Syd's description of their time in Bournemouth elaborated on Donald's. "The first thing Don did was to fill up the tub and have a nice bath full of hot water, even though the rules said, 'use no more than six inches of water.'" Syd described one annoying incident: "We used to go to a little place called Christchurch just for a night out. Often we'd just go into a coffee shop. One evening, we were returning with a group of army guys in their jeep. The driver was a Canadian army chap who had met the eight of us from Sudbury having a get-together. He offered to drive us home to Bournemouth. The Canadian military police stopped us because we were going too slow. They made us get out of the jeep and walk to our lodgings. Thank You Canada!!"

As Donald had lots of spare time, he wrote to his sister Jean. These letters, which in tone and content, were decidedly different from the letters to his parents. To "Little One" he wrote:

Well, my sweet, how goes the mighty struggle for existence on that side of the pond that separates our great "love." No doubt you are still the sprouting little glamour girl I "left behind me." Well, so far this has been a heck of a lot of fun, but I am afraid that is not going to last so very long. The food isn't the same as you would get at the Ritz.

Well, how are your little romances coming along? No doubt by this time the great Con is but a memory, or is he? You must tell me more about yourself. You can now, as I am not in a very advantageous position to tell tales at home. Incidentally, how is that cute roommate of yours from Oakville?

Say, are you a complete blonde yet? I think you should go all the way and pour that whole bottle of peroxide on your noggin. If there is any little thing, (besides a man) you would like me to pick you up over here let me know. Besides, I owe you a birthday present since you knit me that sweater for mine.

Well, so far there has been little excitement with the exception the subs made [cut out by sensor] passes at us and the odd mine is floating around. But don't say anything at home about that. I think they worry enough as it is.

Well, Sexy, this is an English boat, and as you know, Englishmen must have their tea and as it is a quarter to four it is near tea-time, which all adds up to the fact that I must close this letter. Anyway, I'm boring the censor. Well good night, pet? Luff, D C Plaunt Esq.

Chapter 5: Heading Overseas

Now that Donald was overseas, Jean became a more regular correspondent and gave him the news about family and events. Her first letter contained news we'd all love to hear. The Maple Leafs beat the Red Wings for the Stanley Cup after losing the first three games. She returned a clever retort after Donald delivered one of his demeaning comments: "I'm still not the little glamour girl you and everyone left behind. At least being my brother, you don't have to say that I'm just a hang-over from the gold rush."

Jean's letter was the first one he received, and he quickly responded. Life in the resort town it appeared wasn't much different than on board:

> Incidentally, I am having a real soft time of it here. All I have to do is to go to 2 roll calls a day and then sit around for the rest of the time enjoying myself. It costs a lot of money, but we are being paid $4.00 a day for doing nothing. We are billeted in a swank apartment hotel at this former renowned summer resort. In a few days, I get a week's leave when I expect to go up to London and see some of the <u>old</u> sights.
>
> Outside my window, a big Wellington bomber flew by on what I guess is a daylight raid into France. We see a lot of aircraft around here but no Germans. We have had two or three air raid alarms, but the "Jerries" haven't bombed this actual town lately. We can hear bomb explosions every now and again, but I have <u>seen</u> no <u>great</u> damage.
>
> As for the English girls and the way they dance, all I can say is "Phooey!" I haven't seen a decent pair of legs since I left good old Canada! Look here, Baby, you would sure be a queen if you were over here. My god, if you are seen dancing cheek to cheek with a woman over here you are expected to marry her the next morning.

OK, now about your gadding about! Giving old Con the run around, eh? I certainly wish I had my Chevy here. It certainly would be a swell looking buggy over here. I wonder how Helen is getting along with it. I bet it will curb cruise just from habit! I hope the gas rationing isn't too strict. There is only 1 gallon a week here to just certain people.

In looking at the last string of pictures of yourself you sent me, I find they don't do you justice so how's about another string or two of good ones!! You could slip in a snap of that roommate of yours that dropped me a line. I almost forgot what she looked like, except she was darned attractive and had a super personality. In other words, she's OK.

Holy cow – 12 pages – what must I have said? Write soon and often and remember to give me all the dirt, and remember, keep your nose clean.

With a week's leave coming up he hoped the time away would break up the routine. Given that England was in the midst of a war he expressed his surprise at what he was observing to his father: "You would no more guess there is a war in this town than you would in Sudbury except for the uniforms on the streets. The place is 100% intact, and I have yet to see a German aircraft. We get the odd air-raid alarm, but you don't even hear the aircraft motors." In the meantime, he headed off on a seven-day leave.

With all this spare time he became frustrated as he expressed to his father: "I seem to be a professional bum. I expect to be flying in a twin-engine night fighter. However, they will do what they want with me, and I am afraid it won't be for weeks. He commented on the upcoming plebiscite over compulsory enlistment in Canada and echoed his father's views

Chapter 5: Heading Overseas

that a "mighty rush to the farm will commence. If the votes he will draw over here are any sign I would say there was to be conscription." However, Donald was surprised by the attitude of the English people regarding the recruitment issue: "They don't know why we come over and when we tell them there isn't even compulsory service they can't figure us out. They sure have a weird outlook on the whole situation. They are calm all right, but I would say too calm. Propaganda is knee deep around here. Why they even have Mack King built up as a true and loyal statesman (!!!) It sure makes one laugh."

He expressed his appreciation for letters: "Agnes sent a pretty nice photo of Sandy - I've had two letters from her, one from Jeanie and two from Mom, so I am not averaging too bad. No packages as yet, but will be looking forward to them. Keep that mob writing as mail is the big thing over here. Everybody smokes and drinks until 10:00 pm then everything shuts right down."

A Box of Lauras

He asked his mother if she had received her portion of his military allowance from the government. He missed her garden as he hadn't seen many in England. Helen had informed him she was sending him a favourite treat. "I will certainly be glad to sink a tooth into a Laura (Secord) again." Donald added an order to his mother's letter; "a whole chicken (canned), lots of Chateau and Kraft cheeses, jam and lots of chewing gum as I like it to fly with it and it can't be obtained over here." And, "get my camera mad sister to take some around the house, car, etc. and send them."

> HELEN PLAUNT No Date RECEIVED CHOCOLATES THANKS A MILLION ANOTHER HOLIDAY IN LONDON BE GOOD DONALD PLAUNT

It was the first of the countless number of Lauras he would receive. Helen's gift inspired a comical response: "Allo my dear 'elen! And how goes the Titanic struggle with you, my beautiful sister? No doubt you still have Sudbury at your feet (and still nothing to do)! ... no doubt since you now have a car they have elevated you to vice-president or general manager, well, office manager at least." He inquired about the car, commenting: "that crock can really curb cruise[12]... Don't tell the *Mater* or the *Pater* but I think English women stink. The women are 95% lousy, and the other 5% don't give the Canadians a tumble, so figure it out. I just finished my leave, on which, I behaved like a perfect gentleman, all the time ... Drop me a word or two."

Amused that they were "having war games here and that one group just captured the house across the street," he told his mother, "It reminded me of the time I used to run around playing cowboys and Indians." That same day he wrote his father to justify why he was spending so much money: "Doing nothing is the most expensive thing I know. Shows, bus rides and all that sort of stuff. However, I guess I will exist!" In his letter to his father of April 19, he remarked about what he saw as a major British problem:

> Well, about the drinking, Well, I admit <u>everybody</u> over here has a beer or two to be sociable, but it doesn't bother me a bit. I bet there are five fellows in RAF Bournemouth that don't drink. For me, it's a habit to refuse a drink, so I don't have any trouble. As a matter of fact every man, woman and child over 12 has their glass of beer and cigarette.
>
> As for flying with a hangover – a lot fly half-oiled and occasionally get away with it alive. But most drinking is done when the flights are all over. Also, don't worry

---

12 Slang for driving your car around town looking for a pick-up

about me and the "fair sex." You really flatter them over here when you call them "fair."

Although this is Sunday, it seems the same as any other day around here. Today there are manoeuvres going on and firecrackers are being exploded, everybody running around waving guns and a smoke screen laid down. The building across the street is fortified so I expect a pitched battle to be going on under my window any time now.

Two days later he updated his mother:

Kae's box arrived yesterday morning, and it certainly was a sight for sore eyes. They started a little ground school here, but it was a bit boring, so I skipped the rest ... There is talk about us going to the army for a couple of weeks, not so much for the training but to watch the Army in manoeuvres. Tomorrow, I am going to cast my vote to release King on his non-conscription promise. I guess that should go through, and we will be able to hook the odd Frenchman. There was a Sudbury Star in that box Kae sent, and I bet I have read it all thro' twice. How about some more of them. The lack of news makes me close.

In his last letter from Bournemouth, he wrote to his mother: "Not a lot to say but am writing to keep me in the habit as <u>you</u> know, it is a very easy habit to lose. I haven't received any mail the last couple of days because it all comes in groups after a convoy gets in. "Two days later he wrote to her again: "I went by bus to Southampton yesterday and had a look-see at the damage done by Jerry and found it was considerable. However, they haven't been over for over a year. I had a Coca-Cola yesterday, and it really hit the spot. Today I hired a bike and went for a short spin in the country." He was bored. Not only had he not seen a German aircraft, but bemoaned he would be "stuck here for another couple of months."

He was hoping to get presents sent for his Dad and his sister Kae's birthdays which were coming up in April. Given that it would be Easter the following weekend he was thinking about going to church Easter Sunday. He asked for a picture folder to place photos of the house, car and "our younger generation as they come along." Fortunately, his boredom was over, and Donald left for an advanced training session.

CHAPTER 6
Adjusting to a New Way of Life
(MAY 1 - MAY 25, 1942)

"It seems very strange but hardly a day passes that I don't give that rogues gallery[13] of mine a going over."

One of the unexpected benefits of being stationed in Britain was that Donald would get the opportunity to see more of the country that he had visited two years ago. As well as being stationed around the country, he would be granted leave every six weeks. While waiting in Bournemouth, he had a seven-day leave, so he went to visit Bill Lane, who was now with a fighter training squadron south of London. On his way back Donald stopped in London to see the former Sudbury Y director, Joe Barratt. Having a familiar face in the sea of anonymity would make Donald's adjustment flow more smoothly. As head of a branch of the London Y, Barratt would also be a communication hub for all the Sudbury boys, and most were now checking in with him when they were in the British capital. Donald had lunch with his former Ridley teacher and European tour leader, now Major John Page, who had an administrative position with the Canadian Army. Donald was able to get news from him about his many Ridley friends who were now in Britain.

---

13   A wallet of family photos

Blind Landing

Donald was now at Dishforth, an RAF base north-west of the city of York, to take a course in blind landing. This base had been created in 1936 and was used to train recruits and serve as an operations base for Bomber Command. The training unit, known as an Operational Training Unit (OTU), was to train pilots for multi-engine aircraft, using specialized instrument techniques for night flying. This skill was essential as Donald would be flying, primarily at night, in a bomber stream with hundreds of other aircraft towards a target hundreds of kilometres into enemy territory. This course would be the beginning of an additional 250 hours of flying time, along with classroom work, before he would be ready for operations.

After his arrival at the base, he updated his parents and set a goal:

> I am doing a radio blind flying training course and have found it very fascinating. You can land an airplane without seeing a single landmark by using radio and instruments. The only fellow I know here is a Texan who trained with me at Goderich and Brantford. There are darn nice quarters here – it was occupied by Air Force guys and their families in peacetime - there is even a fireplace. They treat us well, and the food is good. My big ambition is to get on four-engine heavy bombers that you would have to see to appreciate. They have them here on this station, but I am afraid I don't rate one just yet. However, when I do get flying on "Ops" I still have my hopes.

He mentioned that he had received a parcel from Kae, but had not received any mail for the last three weeks as he suspected it had been held up in London. A day later, he received letters from both parents and enjoyed hearing about the Easter gathering: "I'll bet those three kids are getting to be an awful gang," he wrote his mother: "Dad says they are growing, and they will soon be having their fights ... The food here is excellent - by excellent, I mean for this country - in the past five days I have had six eggs." He liked the tidbits that he was getting from home and stated that they were: "just the cream of the crop ... I have been bragging to the boys about Canadian chocolates – particularly Lauras – and I can see where I have talked me out of a lot because they are just waiting for a box to come so they can help themselves. I gave quite a bit of my stuff away (food he brought with him), and it certainly was welcome over here. – Ah yes, before I forget – send canned butter whenever you can – it is very handy. We flying crews are very lucky – we can buy extras – like orange juice. One almost feels like a cad being able to walk into the station grocery store and buying that, but, *C'est la guerre*."

> Telegram - LETTERS RECEIVED MANY THANKS PARCELS RECEIVED MANY THANKS LOVE DONALD PLAUNT

He followed his appreciative telegram up with a letter to his mother:

> Marion and your box arrived. I needn't tell you how those "dainties" go around here. Where I'm quartered now is ideal for having feeds. We have a little fireplace in my room and we make toast and tea and use all the trimmings - a grand time is had by all. I don't need to tell you, but the English lads sure don't mind helping me [cut out][14] with the goods. So far I have received K #1, M #1 and Mom #1. No candy from Agnes as you mentioned. Perhaps it was stolen in the mail. That often happens if the package appears to look like chocolates or

---

14 Censors read every letter and cut out any sensitive military information.

cigarettes. Oh yes, in your next one, put in a little peanut butter, please.

I was happy to hear you had the old shin-dig as per usual at Easter. I wish you had a snap of the whole Plaunt clan together. It seems very strange but hardly a day passes that I don't give that rogues gallery (photos of his family) a going over. It is nice to have.

I haven't heard from Bill Lane in over two weeks and Syd in over a week but expect to hear soon.

I am doing what little flying I can in kites known as the Airspeed Oxford. All I am doing is learning how to approach and land on radio without seeing a thing on the ground. The course ends this coming Sunday, and I hope to get to stay here, instead of Bournemouth, even with its nightlife.

Well, Mom, I am going to go have a bath now, have my nights' repast and pull my "little Buggs Plaunt" act, in other words, "hit the hay." Will write in a day or two.

His father asked Donald how he liked England. But instead of talking about England, he wrote about Canada: "Well I like it well enough for the job at hand, but it can't hold a match to Canada as far as I am concerned. I think after the war, if we have a decent government, we will be able to lick the "French Canadian problem." I know an awful lot of Englishmen that trained over there are wanting to go back. If the government makes any offer, we could get all kinds of good people over there." He preferred Dishforth because in Bournemouth: "Our troops have committed more crimes over here than anyone else. Nearly every day there is some holdup committed by them. The people fail to remember we have more forces

Chapter 6: Adjusting to a New Way of Life

over here than any other dominion, and so they figure the Canadians are just a bad lot."

Three of Donald's 'Rogues Gallery' that
he carried in his photo wallet

Top: *Donald's Parents, Mildred and WB*
Bottom left: *Guy, Guy Jr. and Marion Mahaffy*
Bottom right: *Bill, Sandra and Agnes Plaunt*

An Unexpected Article in the Press

Jean had sent Donald a newspaper clipping regarding his pink teddy bear that greatly upset him. He justified the circumstances that led to it to his father: "Zounds! I didn't think that would be in. I gave the Canadian Press reporter my name and home address so that you would learn when I arrived. I then got talking to him and found he knew Bill Austin, and finally I mentioned the bear, and consequently that horrible write-up." Donald got the announcement of the safe arrival conveyed to his family, but the reporter added a few details that embarrassed him: "A pink teddy bear was the magic that protected D. C. Plaunt of Sudbury Ontario from all evil. It was slightly battered from being carried from one training camp after another but retained the look of a beneficent Buddha." Despite all the derogatory nonsense he used to tease Jean he told his father: "I guess you are rather right about her growing up pretty nice. I guess she is the good looking one in your family, but she is going to have to do some stepping to beat that auburn headed niece of mine." He mentioned that he was finding the course on "Blind Approach Landing" difficult but "it is really a marvelous training."

In his next letter to his mother, Donald commented on a speech Churchill had given the night before about the optimistic prospects for the war now that the United States was their ally. He added his opinion on the new bombers: "I know now we have by far the best aircraft. Particularly our bombers. The four-engine ones are marvelous." Four days later he wrote to her:

> As you can see by the heading, I am still at [cut out] doing absolutely nothing, but sightseeing. I am with Air Control and at this minute I am supposedly on duty, but as I have nothing to do, I have time to write you.
>
> Helen wrote me that you hadn't received any of my letters yet. That amazes me as I am sure I have averaged

Chapter 6: Adjusting to a New Way of Life

at least four a week to you and Dad. The only explanation I can see is that they are held up by the censor. Your mail is uncensored, so perhaps that is why I receive yours in better time than you receive mine. Incidentally, did Dad get that pipe I sent home for him for his birthday? I don't like to say this, but I figure there could be something fishy going on somewhere in the mail. I presume this as I have not to date received any of the boxes of chocolates you sent. The other boxes, yours, Kae's and Marion's all arrived here. It just makes one think and wonder what happened. I will feel much better when my mail has been getting to you regularly.

> <u>May 16 '42</u> - sans origin - WB PLAUNT STILL KICKING HAVE YOU RECEIVED MUCH MAIL FROM ME YOU SENT UNIFORM WRITE OFTEN DONALD PLAUNT

Two days later, he expressed the importance of mail to his father: "No new letters but will write what news I have. I received a note from Agnes, and she said you were receiving my first letters at the time (Apr. 24). Next to you and Mom, Agnes has written the most, much appreciated. So help me, a letter is as good as a steak dinner, and I haven't had one of those since Halifax." He asked about the effects of gas rationing on his business and wondered how his "old Lassie" (his car) was running. "The roads over here are deserted as I'll bet ½ million cars have been "grounded" completely since I have arrived here. However, the gas over here is used for a real good purpose. I have learned the real "gin" on all the big raids, Paris, Rostock, etc. I only wish I could write and tell you the actual figures as I had them presented, but unfortunately, I can't. But I can say that Germany is in for far worse than she ever handed to us. That is no eyewash either."

On Leave

He was granted leave for a few days and visited some ancient ruins nearby. He commented on a party that he was missing: "All the boys are over in the Mess having a little stag party which is nothing but a beautiful drunk. By the time it ends they can hardly crawl home to bed. Not appearing to be preaching, but I don't figure it is any too pleasant a sight to see them all boozing so, for my sake, I am glad I am on the "wagon." It may sound silly coming from me, but if you could see, this goes on. Well, I have shot my bolt for now so I will close. Look after yourself, and of course, the grandchildren, etc."

He was in a cheerful mood after he received some letters. On May 19, he wrote to his mother:

> I was extremely glad to hear from you, along with a box of Lauras and a box of foodstuffs. Very nice indeed. While I am on the subject of food, I have an apology to make. That canned chicken I presumed was "no good" is definitely OK. I had my first can last night, and I enjoyed it. Even so, I wouldn't mind one of those whole ones. I hear that the kids are constant squawkers. I hope I get some more snaps of them as if I don't, I won't be able to recognize them. I was thinking about their birthdays and Christmas gifts. If I am all paid up out of the $21 a month that is supposed to be yours, could you put $10 in the bank for them on each occasion?

In the second letter from his mother that day she had told him about the IODE's attempt to raise funds for a new airplane. Donald wrote back; "Make that a Stirling for me, eh." He was also happy to hear that Canadian Pacific was decorating the railway station in Sudbury: "It is certainly time they painted that CP station. It is surprising the number of

Chapter 6: Adjusting to a New Way of Life

boys I have run into that have a very dull opinion of Sudbury just because all they had seen was that dingy station."

He frequently requested family photos and commented on their importance to him: "I enjoyed that photo of Grandma and Grandpa together. It takes things like that to bring back the good old days, and I'll bet the ones of the "infant army" were swell too. I got a bunch of snaps from Billy and for the last six hours, I have been going around laughing every time I think of the expressions on their faces. They certainly take the cake." About his attempt to take photos of himself he wrote: "You got to have the subject to work on first. Maybe as you say, if ever I get the king's commission I will have some decent ones taken over here."

He was also appreciative of the parcels that had arrived, such as more chocolates from Helen and clothing from his mother. About the deal with his father, he wrote to his mother: "So Father tried to get you to trick me to smoke, eh. Tell him in another year or so maybe. But seriously, that was an excellent idea as cigarettes, particularly good ones like the Canadian brands, are rather scarce, and I wished I had brought some with me to give to my friends who smoke. I certainly hope that the Laura Secord shop doesn't close as I am fond of their chocolates. And I hope to keep getting them." He knew how to drop a hint.

His mother told Donald that his young neighborhood friends had asked about him. His response: "You can inform that mighty mob that lives around there, Hinds (Ozzie and Jim), Ted Smith, and Crangs (John and Don) that if they expect me to write them, they will have to write first and give me their addresses. Not that I have too much time but they are a darn good gang of kids." He ended with: "Still doing nothing is a pleasant way of getting paid for it and having our service time mount up. Tomorrow is my 1st anniversary of being in the RCAF and the same date my second monthly anniversary of being in "Jollie" England. Let's have more of those nice long eight-pagers from you."

After hearing from Bill about the affairs in his lumber camp, Donald expressed his concern about Bill's involvement in the war to his father:

In spite of the great interest Bill is taking in the business, he is itching to get into this mess. Don't mention this to him, but I know you're the reason he isn't. Well, keep on being it, as there is no darn sense in him joining at all. This may sound darn strange to hear me preaching like an old man, but this is one angle I have a better see at. He is doing more and better work for the advancement of this war than I or 95% of others who are ballyhooed. 50% of the Armed Forces work while 50% make themselves useful by being a great reserve for the Big Show. Please don't say anything to him, but keep him out and the brothers-in-law as well. For men in their professions it is just a burden and an extra load for those at home. Bill takes a look at his school friends etc. and figures he should be for it too. But they haven't a family and are not connected with a war industry as he is.

Glad to hear Guy and Mac are busy and are working hard. I got a bunch of snaps of their families and are those children ever coming along. The boys I show the pictures to claim that Andy and Guy both look a little like me. I guess though they just have that "Plaunt" look about them. Not so Sandy, though, she is to be the good looking one.

What kind of plane is Mother trying to help the IODE buy? Is it a national campaign or what? I think Mom likes doing that sort of work although it is hard.

Donald mentioned Paul Molson, one of his father's employees whom he had a "great deal of respect for his judgment since the night at Wye he told you and me that Russia and Germany would divide up Poland, and that was a year before it happened." He added some unkind words about his Canadian prime minister: "I was certainly pleased when I heard the results of the plebiscite and disgusted to an extreme when an aluminum plant in that certain province had to be closed due to that rush to the farm (hiding from recruiters) you predicted. I, too, am waiting with interest to see just what our noble Willie K (PM) will do. The first thing I hope would be that he would resign, but that is just a dream." He reassured his father:

> You needn't worry about me as I am not doing a lot flying at present. However, today I had the pleasure of going up in a [several lines cut out] When I compare their aircraft with ours I can see where we have superior and quality aircraft. I think Germany is in for a terrible walloping [cut out] ... Henry Ford is doing a pretty good job on his own. I hope his bombers are a little better than his cars were.

On May 28, 1942, Donald wrote to his parents from a city he was becoming very familiar with:

> This is London calling! You guessed it; I am on leave again. Granted because there is nothing for us to do in Dishforth. The American kid that was with me got his leave a few days before I did and so I made the fatal mistake of coming to London alone. For the biggest city in the world, it is certainly the most lonesome if one is on the loose alone.
>
> However, tomorrow I am leaving here. I am going to spend the rest of my vacation in Devon. I am staying with one of the members of Lady Francis Ryders' organization. I picked Devon because that is supposed to be the real nice spot in England at this time. Also, I am very

curious to see Mr. Morris again. You remember my Ridley housemaster who joined up just three days before I did. He is an L.A.C. (Leading Aircraftman) on radio work. There is another fine example of our RCAF commissions. If anyone I know deserves one, he certainly does and yet! It certainly peeves a person. However, I see where our friend Mr. Powers (Minister of National Defence for Air) is holding out for commissions for all aircrew; I wish him luck.

I am staying at the hotel that our gang stayed at in '39. It certainly brings back the fondest of memories. Every time I see Major Page, we just shovel back and forth about the trip.

20th Birthday

On his 20th birthday, he wrote to his mother from Exeter, the major city in Devon:

> What is so rare as a day in June, particularly June first. Why it is as rare as 1 in 365 which really aren't bad odds. That one year to go means that our Dear Father is going to quit buying Victory Bonds and slip yours truly a little cash for our deal (not to drink or smoke). As a matter of fact, I fully expect to be home to collect. In other words, I think the mighty 3rd Reich is on, what is commonly known as the "downgrade." A few more nights at 1,000+ bombers over a few of their pet cities and I will be dreadfully surprised if there isn't the odd word of peace floating from the lips of our eloquent wall-painter (Hitler).

Chapter 6: Adjusting to a New Way of Life

As you are wondering from my letterhead what am I doing in Exeter? I must explain that in spite of the all out RAF effort they found it necessary to give this great personality another week's leave. I guess they figure my lying in bed until 11:00 am, getting up, doing absolutely nothing, called air control, and then going back to bed, as being too hard on the nerves, so here I am.

I am staying with Dr. and Mrs. Canley, who are the very nicest of people. Exeter has just been blitzed, and so there is no night life, but that suits me quite all right. Strange as it may seem, the next door neighbours to the Canleys are people by the name of Capenev who have two girls in Canada attending Branksome. A pretty small world isn't it? I was very glad to see Mr. Morris again. I went to see him at his station near here. Then the Canleys had him in for a little visit. He is an exceptional fellow whom I admire very much.

Exeter is in very much of a shambles, and it was a case of the Jerries bombing an entirely non-military objective. It seems so strange that the little he does raid this country that he would waste his bombs on targets useless to him. I honestly think that things look bright, although by the time this reaches you, an entire change might have come over the situation.

I brought the 5 lb. box of chocolates Helen sent me down to Exeter with me. Are the people ever crazy for them. I don't think they would trade them for their weight in gold. Of course, I am getting my nose in on the deal too.

I guess today your garden will just be coming into its glory. By the time this reaches you the old raspberries will be on their way. Eat an extra dish of them for me, eh? I haven't heard of your summer plans. You must let me in on your deep dark secret.

Your loving son Donald C

While on leave he sent one telegram.

> June 5 '42 - HARROGATE — CP Telegraphs EVERYTHING ALRIGHT LOVE. DONALD PLAUNT

CHAPTER 7

A Soothing Cup of Tea

(MAY 26 - JULY 29, 1942)

"The weather here has been terrible. More fog and miserable drizzle than you would see in 10 years at home. I know now why the English are such tea drinkers. Even I have to nip in and get a cup every few hours to get the dampness out of my system."

Lousy Weather

His new base was at Little Rissington in the Cotswolds, a picturesque area of rolling hills and an unusual place for an airfield. He was excited about his new base and wanted to tell his mother: "We are here in the Cotswolds which you know are beauty features of England. I often thought of how you would like to take a walk down one of their highways, which are about as wide as our lane, looking over the land and scenery. It is very charming, but I am afraid this country runs a poor second to Canada."

But, as beautiful as Little Rissington appeared to Donald, it was wet. All the time. What would have been a beautifully sunny summer in Canada felt more like October there. In a brief note to his mother, he elaborated: "The weather here has been terrible. More fog and miserable drizzle than you would see in 10 years at home. At times, I would have thought you would like this country and then I am positive you wouldn't. I know now why the English are such tea drinkers. Even I have to nip in and get a cup every few hours to get the dampness out of my system."

The weather can get you down, and the English weather was doing just that to Donald. But there were other reasons for his melancholy. He was no longer with Syd, and he was a stranger among those who did not know him, and this estrangement began to affect him.

Inactivity also contributed to his moodiness. As best as the RAF was trying to accommodate his flying needs, there were hundreds of other fresh aircrew coming from Canada every time a convoy landed. Individual needs were secondary. So inactivity, lack of contact with friends and family, along with lousy weather contributed to a slight case of homesickness. With few friends and no family to cheer him up, Donald longed to be where he felt most comfortable. He was in limbo, but at least he was getting an opportunity here and there to take a course, get some leave, and advance to what he was here for - to fly one of those big bombers. His time would come. Sometimes, Donald resorted to complaining in his letters, and there was no shortage of topics.

RAF Grumblings

One objection Donald expressed to his father was about leaves:

> One is almost able to scrounge a few days leave over here as easy as rolling off a log. When we were in Canada, where we could have had a darn good time, they handed out leave as if it was seriously jeopardizing the war effort if they gave us an extra day or two. Also, I certainly miss my little car. If you want to get anywhere over here, you either walk or stand up on a bus while you are travelling. Another fine behaviour one notices over here is that you never see an Englishman give his seat to a woman on a bus. And the line we are fed about their manners.

Chapter 7: A Soothing Cup of Tea

There was one issue that bothered Donald more than any other - the RAF promotion policy. He felt rather humble with the rank of sergeant pilot. One sensed some envy at his peers who were promoted such as his good friend from Ridley he had travelled with to Europe in 1939. To his mother, he wrote: "I see by the *Acta* that Bill Squire is now a 2nd Lieut. His Dad did want him to get one pretty bad. To tell the truth, that is the big number one reason that I would like to have one as well." On a recent visit to see Bill Lane, Donald learned that Bill had received a minor promotion to flight sergeant. Donald had become accustomed to his plight and admitted that his life as a sergeant pilot was pretty good. But given his expectations, from being 2IC of the Ridley Cadet Corps, he felt he was officer class material. However, it was the recent change in promotion policy that upset him as he wrote to his father:

> That brings me around to the time-worn subject of promotion. I guess Syd and I find ourselves in a bad spot. Until now, RCAF persons both at home and in service overseas, automatically become a flight sergeant in 6 months. Then this big announcement was given out seven months ago by your political friends, that they would commission all pilots. But instead of things getting any better, they are now worse. The set-up now is that the noble airmen at home are promoted quickly due to the extreme danger of their work and great responsibility of flying an Anson worth all of $25,000 to $50,000. I must agree that it is only correct, while fellows like myself – and there are hundreds – have only the responsibility of a $250,000 Lancaster and the hide of 6 other men on our hands – should wait one year to make the mighty jump.
>
> The Yankees probably aren't doing so hot as an Air Force, but they know how to treat their aircrews. All of

their pilots are officers. They would not think of having a captain of their four-engine aircraft a lowly sergeant, but I guess I am a member of the RAF, so a sergeant I remain. To make matters a lot worse, American fellows who were sergeants in Canada are transferring back to the US Forces, and they immediately become officers.

Well, that is off my chest. Please don't say any of this to anyone else. I wouldn't write anything like this only I feel pretty punk today. You know how a day will get you bad. When I enquired and found out, that if I had accepted an instructor's job at home, I would have received a promotion 3 ½ months ago. Somehow I figure it should be the other way around. But again, I could be wrong, eh? Well, that's a load off of my chest now to quit complaining and to get on with a bit of narrative that is not all moaning.

Donald frequently railed at the promotion policy, but since he was in the RAF, it was not about to change. For the British, the underlying criterion was class. Most, if not all, officers came from the educated or higher social class which usually meant having a public school education. "You had to be a gentleman," as one author put it. For the Americans and the newly formed RCAF Group, the key criterion was merit. They believed highly trained personnel like pilots and navigators deserved the recognition. This one issue may have contributed to Donald's disenchantment with the RAF and his desire to return home after completing his tour of duty.

Not all agreed with making a pilot a different class than the crew. Canadian Lancaster pilot, Douglas Harvey, believed the success of a bomber crew depended on them working as a close-knit team. Not only did they work together, but they also lived in a Nissen hut, and they ate and socialized together in a sergeants' mess. Once someone in the crew

Chapter 7: A Soothing Cup of Tea

earned a promotion, he no longer ate or lived with his mates. An officer lived in upscale quarters, ate in a better mess and received double the pay. There was one officer in Donald's crew, Alex Smith, but there is little mention of him in his letters because Donald only saw him when they were flying. Donald's comments (in a later chapter) demonstrated that he liked his crew and was getting to know them in their living quarters where they hung out together. Being an officer may have satisfied Donald's ego and his expectations, but he may have lost something in return.

News from Home

Donald could always have a soothing cup of tea to offset the damp weather, but he was unable to deal with the promotion policy except to complain. However, there was one thing that always brightened his spirits, and it usually happened whenever he returned from leave. As he expressed to his father:

> I just returned from leave on the 3rd and found a stack of mail, including your letter of May 15th and your cable. You said I must be thinking of home! You certainly hit the nail on the head there. It doesn't help one's spirit just sitting around when there are 1,000 bombers a night going over. It makes one very restless. However, we are not doing anything. I have to get up at 2 am and go to the control tower. It is the Air Ministry's orders that a qualified pilot is on the ground while kites are landing.
>
> The big bomber offensive is really a marvelous show: it is a masterpiece of organization.
>
> Jean sent me some amazing snaps of the family on Easter Sunday. They certainly were nice to get. I don't suppose

I need to remind you that this is my last year as a non-smoker. It doesn't seem like five years we swung that deal does it? Tonight I managed to get a super beef steak and did it ever hit the spot. Don't misunderstand me that we are not well fed. I weigh as much now or more than I ever did.

The Sudbury Stars are reaching me all OK, and I read them carefully. Mr. Miller (his father's closest friend) seems to be having a pretty tough time in the courts these days. And how is your golf game? You have made no mention of your endeavours at the royal and ancient game.

The only thing I am flying now is Dat bird de Link. It gets tedious but is very good to keep you on the bit. Talking of fronts, I think that an awful lot will depend on the outcome of the Libya campaigns. (Montgomery vs. Rommel) I certainly hope we can drive Jerry right out of there completely.

With the two-hour daylight saving time over here the evenings are becoming extremely long. It is 11:11 and the sun is just setting. It makes it very tricky if one wants to get to bed early. Now I am going to have a bath and hit the hay so I will end this sad epistle.

After receiving a letter from Jean, he reminded her of his expectations. "For a minute, I was afraid that your right arm had been badly injured. But you sure made a comeback; two letters arrived here together." He covered many topics; his appreciation for the snaps she enclosed; his envy that she was going home for the summer holiday; his hope that Jean would be a prefect in her last year at Branksome and that one day she would become a "voice" at Queen's Park. But most of all, he hoped she would do well in school for another reason. "No need to mention how proud Dad and Mom would be, and take it from me, they are <u>the</u> <u>two</u> that count." However, he was disappointed he hadn't received his birthday sweater she had promised him, "Maybe next June 1st, eh?"

Jean's return letter reported on the ongoing rift between their father and Helen because they "are so strong headed they don't exactly live peacefully." Jean felt Helen needed to get out of town and go to Toronto to defuse the stand-off. As well, Helen was no longer able to drive his car because of gas rationing. Jean wrote him that she was sorry to "hear that the legs over there aren't very good. I am enclosing a photo of a pair I hope will do. Not mine, of course."

In a letter to his mother, he thanked her for the cigarettes for his buddies. He mentioned that he had received a letter from Mac (Kae's husband) who had received a cable from his father in China. The Japanese were about to expel Rev. Thomson and other foreign missionaries from China. The remainder were interred in POW camps for the rest of the war, including Mac's sister, Betty, and her husband, Dr. Geoffrey Gale. Two days later he wrote his father just to "keep the ball rolling." He mentioned that Syd Smith would be coming to see him in a few days: "I certainly miss him a lot. I do as I am the only Canadian stationed here and at times it becomes somewhat lonesome. But seeing I'm a big boy now, I don't let that worry me too much." Syd had heard from Bill Lane that he was doing well. Donald was in contact with a couple of their Sudbury friends, Eddy McMitchell, who was in the Air Force, and Art Cressy, who was in the Grey and Simcoe Foresters with some other Sudbury boys. He hoped to see them soon.

Donald did not discuss his personal beliefs very often, but an incident at home prompted him to reveal his views to his mother:

> The Edwards' fire was entire news to me. Things like that make me believe an awful lot in fatalism. I shouldn't call it fatalism, but I should say that things are happening the

way they do or happen the way they do for some reason. Look how long they were married without any children. If they had their son at the ordinary time, he would likely be my age or older and would maybe be away from home over here or elsewhere. Then who would they have had to wake them up in time to get out? My idea is that people are created and die at pre-determined times.

Although he joked about this philosophy being "silly," his comments reflected his underlying beliefs. How else could these young men - many of them teenagers - go into battle without believing they had a chance to survive? Some believed they were invincible, while others, like Syd, told me, he just didn't think about it. Others were so overcome with fear, they had to quit and were disgraced and branded with the LMF (lacking moral fiber) label. Donald felt awkward disclosing his beliefs and requested that his mother not "show this silly letter to anyone else, as there are perhaps some very stupid statements in it that would sound phony to anyone else."

Donald expressed to his mother how appreciative he was of his sisters: "So glad Jeanie is getting around a little more now and going to the prep school dances. She is a good kid and deserves a lot. Funny how you don't appreciate people when you are with them, isn't it? ... I hope Helen isn't holding back on the car. After all, it's hers now, isn't it? I received Kae's box today, her Number Two. It is very nice indeed."

On a four-day leave, he visited Syd and went horseback riding and blamed a "spirited hunter" for making his arm stiff. When he returned, he found a letter from his mother and one from Jim Hinds, his young neighbourhood friend who had inherited his goalie pads. His birthday box had arrived, and he especially enjoyed "my birthday cake and it was pip of a one." Although he was pleased with some of the items, he sent her a shopping list for more items he wanted. "I hope you have sent my duffle bag by now as it will certainly come in handy. I am glad you have sent the khaki shirts. I wish you would send me a bottle of calamine lotion as I am still working on the old face. My skin is not bad now. You could

Chapter 7: A Soothing Cup of Tea

slip in a few chocolate bars into your packages. Also, I have not seen many Lauras of late." He also announced he was moving to a new base for additional training.

Mail governed Donald's mood. If he got lots, he was up; if little, he was down. His mother received the brunt of his complaints, and it must surely have bothered her, not so much because he was complaining, but how it reflected his state of mind. Rationally, he knew there were reasons for the mail not getting through, but emotionally he found it trying. On his arrival at his new base, Little Rissington on June 25th, he wrote to her. "It is pretty maddening writing very often and not getting very much answered." He also admitted it may have been because of his change of address and that he was exhausted having to be up at 4:00 am for his move. But mail wasn't the only factor contributing to Donald's mood - loneliness, inactivity, lack of mail, RAF promotion - also plagued him at times. He just hadn't developed sufficient uppers to offset the downers. Now, that was about to change.

On a more positive note, his letters revealed that he had heard from Eddy McMitchell and hoped to see him on his next leave. He was enjoying his new base: "I am back with the lot I trained with, and I am rather enjoying it here. Dishforth was a super station, but it was rather dead." He complained again about the imbalance of leaves in Britain and Canada, newspapers, the weather, food and wished "I had a couple of parcels or a box of Lauras to work on now." As usual, he closed with his refrain; "Here's hoping that you are often writing and that soon I will get a pile of letters."

His enjoyment of his new base didn't last long, as one week later, he called it a "joint" in a letter to Jean. His main criticism, "Absolutely nothing for miles." However, he was flying several times a day - his log book shows 14 flights from June 26 to June 30 - so there wasn't much free time. He paid her a high compliment: "I envy the way you can write nice long letters and keep 'em interesting. I wish I had the knack." And he liked her photos: "Hey! Who owns those legs? You can tell her for me God sure gave her a gift. They aren't Miss Read, are they? (the elderly Branksome principal)" And he reminded her: "BUT I AM STILL EXPECTING THAT SWEATER FOR JUNE 1ST 1941 !!!!!!!?????!x." It was already one year late.

There was one topic he revealed to Jean that he rarely mentioned to his parents. The fiancé of his former girlfriend, Jeanie Ross, had been killed in a training accident: "It is rather tough luck. A lot of my friends are getting "it" now. One fellow, you must have heard me mention, Tex Elwell from Texas, whom I hung around with, was killed in a mid-air collision lately. All told, 7 of my class have been killed since we reached here. Say nothing to the family about it at all." The remainder of the letter was taken up with teenage chatter about her boyfriends: "I am going to see Snuffy (Syd) this weekend, and I will give him your "luff" and a request for a few ripe jokes. I could send you a couple of stories myself, but the censor might think that you aren't a "lidy." Well, *soeur* puss I must away and take wings a fly, so I'm checking out, *au revoir*."

Birthday Parcels

In mid-June, Donald's birthday parcels started to arrive, and he replied first to Jean:

> Your super box arrived this morning, and it is A+ and then some. I have had an awful urge for bars and gum, and it just fits the ticket. Of course, thank Louise and Gay for their contribution. Also, thanks for the pin. I have it on my battle-dress.
>
> PS Get that camera of yours going and let me have some snaps, eh? Also, don't cut your hair off!

Then to his father:

Chapter 7: A Soothing Cup of Tea

We are quite busy and every second morning we are up at 5:00 am and fly until 10:45 pm. The days are long, and we are getting as much time in as possible while the weather is good. We are flying the Oxford which is a letdown from the Anson.

We are becoming familiarized with the country. Syd is with a training unit He is a bit ahead of me, but I hope to catch up soon. I will get over to see him on leave next weekend."

Donald commented on the deteriorating situation in Egypt after the Germans had captured Tobruk: "I have given up paying any attention to the Egyptian war front as I am rather disappointed at the way it has turned out. But we can still hope for the best."

Despite taking three flights of approximately an hour each on June 30th, he found time to write his mother: "Yesterday a pile of mail came in with two parcels. Among it was your letter sent June 6. Glad to hear everyone is well and enjoying life and that the little car is useful to you. Don't hesitate to use it for fear of wearing it out as I have already made up my mind I will turn it in and with my non-drinking money get me a new convertible. Sounds good, eh?" He finished the letter which read more like a mail order: "I received the birthday parcel, but there were no khaki shirts in it. You could write to <u>Simpson's</u> and get me Air Force blue shirts with detached tab collars at once and forward them, as I am getting rather short of shirts." He was pleased that boxes had arrived from Kae and Bill, both from Simpson's, but added, "I hope someday to get a box with a good choc. cake. Maybe, eh?" and later requested, "You could send concentrated fruit juices, though."

The birthday parcels and letters boosted his spirits. Parcels from Kae, Agnes and Helen arrived along with some peanut butter and new shirts to go with his summer uniform. He had been to see Syd on a 48-hour leave and had received a letter from Bill Lane, whom he hoped to see soon before he headed off to Scotland for his next posting. A week later he told his mother that he had almost finished his night flying course but was more enthusiastic about his copious birthday goodies: "I have been receiving parcels like wild-fire, and it certainly suits me swell. I even got one from a kid in Lower School at Ridley which I must acknowledge right away. The Sudbury Stars are arriving OK as well. I had a nice letter from Marion and Guy yesterday as well as one from Aunt Pearl." And another request: "I think it is a good idea to send the cigs. Don't get me wrong I don't use them yet, but I like the idea of having them to give away. I think I will be glad when the time comes. I will answer #18 tomorrow."

Two days later, on July 10, he told his father that his 10 cent air mail letter had only taken 11 days to reach him. He was: "Glad to hear from you after a silence for a short spell (he was always less critical about a lack of letters from his father). I also received a letter from brother Bill written a couple of days later, and he told me about the dirty trick the men pulled over July 1st holiday. "Wait until peacetime and they will be crawling for jobs." He reassured his father on the risks of flying: "I don't think there is an awful lot to worry about, as there is only a small percentage of the boys getting hurt," which was a very different message from what he had told Jean. He appreciated the letters and parcels as: "they are a Godsend. The food on this station isn't what it was on the last one, so I can use the extra food. Must close now. Write often."

> <u>July 14 '42</u> – Telegram –Great Britain – MRS WB PLAUNT LETTERS AND PARCELS RECEIVED MANY THANKS ALL MY LOVE D PLAUNT

After he had sent the telegram, he wrote to his mother: "Well, it sure is nice getting all kinds of letters, and it sure makes me feel good hearing plenty from you … As regards that picture. I have a sneaking suspicion that I may get a promotion although it is indefinite. I'll have a photo taken then, OK?" He mentioned Syd was now with an OTU (Operational

Training Unit) and Donald expected to be going to one soon. He had another letter from his Ridley friend, Crossie Clark, who told him his brother was in the commandos in Britain. Donald had seen Bill Lane the previous week, and he was looking fine. Given that he was kept busy, he assured his mother that "we don't get a chance to raise Hades, so don't worry."

In a follow-up letter, he wrote to her from the satellite airdrome of Little Rissy with his hopes that: "There is a stack of mail for me when I get back to my base, as I will have to answer them as well. However, I hope to move soon, and there is one consolation, and that is the mess can't be any worse than this one." He added some news: "Had a letter from Syd and he is fine although he has yet to solo on a Hampden, a twin-engine medium bomber. Mr. Morris wrote me that he was considering re-mustering from a wireless operator to a translator. He is pretty "hot" in his languages. Remember he got me my <u>Frenches</u>." He thanked me for the oranges I sent him as they were the first he has had since St. Catharines." It wasn't too often that he mentioned the war situation to his mother, but he told her: "Things are looking bad in North Africa, but I think it is us laying up our pile of defeats before we really lay into them. Then you will hear them hollering."

A Low Point in the War

As Donald experienced a gloomy phase with not much to occupy him, the Allies scorecard was equally unsettling. 1942 was the low point in the war despite the entry of the Americans on December 7, 1941. The Germans and Japanese were winning in every theatre of the war. By the summer, the Japanese were in control of Guadalcanal and had destroyed the British and Dutch Navies in the Pacific. As well, the Germans thwarted the Canadian attack on Dieppe in August, and the Germans were gaining momentum in North Africa as the first battle of El Alamein had begun. In Russia, the German army defeated the Russians at

Sebastopol and was advancing on Stalingrad. The Battle of the Atlantic was also going poorly for the Allies, as the wolf packs were sinking thousands of tons of Allied ships. But, as Donald predicted, things would be improving by the fall.

Donald's next move was east of London, to Wattisham, in Suffolk. He was to take a week course on navigation using a homing method which he could not disclose. He wrote to his father that he had heard from Syd and Bill, and he reported they were both "going strong." Bill was now with a Canadian Spitfire squadron. Donald told him that a Canadian bomber group was being talked about but: "I am not particular whether or not I get on an all-Canadian squadron. They claim that several more are to be formed." He had heard that the Canadians were not getting the heavy bombers like the Lancaster, which he hoped to fly. That was discouraging and meant that Donald's only hope of flying a Lancaster was with an RAF squadron. He was billeted in a: "palatial Nissen hut on a country lane. I hired a bike from a local farmer at sixpence a day so I could get to the airfield easier." He liked it here as: "the mess here is 100% better than the one at Rissy, where I existed on the boxes I got from home. However, don't worry, I still throw my 210 around." All those sweets and food from Canada were indeed having an effect as he was now 20 pounds heavier from when he enlisted 14 months ago, validating the basis for his Ridley nickname.

He returned to Little Rissy on July 29 and completed another exercise on instrument flying. A few days later he told his mother that he had received her telegram and that he was hoping to get some photos of their new summer camp on Pog. He told her that a Canadian padre (clergy) had visited and inquired if there was anything that was bothering him. If there was, Donald didn't mention it. The padre suggested that airmen tell their families not to list items specifically in the parcels, but as "comforts" so as to not tip off would-be thieves. That was vital information Donald could use.

In his letter to his mother on August 7, written at 2:00 am, he was in a good mood, as he had received a: "pile of Canadian mail and a real

Chapter 7: A Soothing Cup of Tea

super-deluxe picture of the 'young-uns' and are they ever cute. I think the most notable change is in Sandy, and it is definitely for the better. Guy is a weird (but cute) looking like a little cuss. I am glad to hear Drew is cracking teeth now, too." He expressed his relief that Mac's father was getting out of China and that despite his reluctance to leave, his departure would relieve the Thomson family.

Although the past several weeks had been a trying time for Donald, he was hopeful that the new posting would lift his spirits. He told his mother that he was pleased that he was heading to Scotland, in his mind, his ancestral home. He was going to an OTU base at Kinloss near the North Sea to train on the Whitley, a two-engine bomber, which would lead to the conversion to a four-engine bomber. He had his heart set on the Lancaster, now considered to be the best aircraft in the British bombing armada. Surprisingly, this information was not cut out, suggesting a slack censor or changing criteria. But there was a precise order to end his last letter from Rissy: "Next time you are in Toronto get a pair of black Oxfords, plain toe-cap and a buckle on them, size ten double E, crepe soles, if possible, and ship them over. I need not tell you to make them good quality ones as you know there is no sense sending ordinary shoes. Will write again soon after I get to my new station next Monday."

CHAPTER 8
A Return to Bonnie Scotland
(AUGUST 8 - OCTOBER 21, 1942)

"I will get another posting to a different type of aircraft. I have my fingers crossed for Lancasters. I will soon know."

In 2003, my wife, Mandy and I visited Scotland, and we included a visit to RAF Kinloss where Donald trained before his selection to a four-engine bomber. Established in 1939 as a training base, Kinloss is on the northern coastline that overlooks the North Sea. When we told the security personnel that my uncle had trained there, we were warmly welcomed and given a tour of the base. At the time of our visit, Kinloss was an airbase for Nimrods, an anti-submarine aircraft patrolling the North Sea for Soviet submarines. In 2010, after the downfall of the Soviet Union, the RAF closed the base.

For a wannabe Scot, Donald would have felt he was returning to his ancestral homeland. After arriving, he wrote to his mother: "I am now up in Scotland, and I certainly like it a lot better than England. The people as well. I live in a beautiful old manor house on a large estate. It is a marvelous old place. A shame that it must be used for billets. A family built it who made [cut out]. Kinloss isn't such a bad station, but it has rained continually since I arrived here."

High Hopes for a Lancaster

This training session would be the defining moment for Donald. At the conclusion of his time here, he would be assigned to one of the new four-engine bombers: the Stirling, Halifax or Lancaster. He felt fortunate that he hadn't advanced as quickly as Syd, who was flying a two-engine Wellington, soon be phased out. Now the four-engine bombers were replacing most of the two-engine ones as quickly as they came off the assembly line. However, even the Stirling was found to be inadequate for the demands of bombing operations and it was relegated to non-bombing functions. The Lancaster and the two-engine Mosquito[15] became the focus of production because of their superior performance. Donald's remark about not wanting to be in a Canadian group reflected his concern that the Canadians would not be flying Lancasters in early 1942. Consequently, he chose to remain with an RAF squadron, despite his complaints, with high expectations he would be selected to fly the "Lanc."

As Donald arrived in Scotland, the Lancaster was coming into active service. Its development was extraordinarily swift, having had its first test flight in early 1941. The initial success was outstanding, primarily because it kept the best features of the Manchester frame, along with some significant upgrades, such as three .303 machine guns and a larger and longer bomb bay door that permitted bigger payloads. It routinely carried a 4,000-pound impact bomb, along with hundreds of incendiaries. Later versions of the Lanc could carry a 22,000 "Grand Slam earthquake" bomb. Most importantly, it was powered by the most reliable engines anywhere - four Rolls-Royce Merlin engines. The Lancaster could fly at 20,000-feet and carry double the bomb load of an American Flying Fortress. Talk among pilots was unanimous: they all wanted to fly it.

---

15 The Mosquito fighter/bomber was the third most exceptional British aircraft as it had the speed-up to 385 mph, a range of 1,800 miles, could carry a 2,000 pound bomb and take on German fighters as well. It became the lead aircraft, or "pathfinder" in front of the bomber stream, assigned to mark the bombing target.

However, as they were just coming on stream, many would have to wait. Would Donald be chosen? He would have to wait until the end of his time at Kinloss to find out.

On his way to Scotland, Donald saw Bill Lane in London, who was delighted with his new Canadian fighter squadron. After arriving at Kinloss, Donald sent a note to his father expressing his pleasure at being in "Bonnie Scotland." His stay in Kinloss would last two and a half months, the longest period he would spend at one base since his arrival in the UK. At this base, all aircrew lived off-base and were dispersed in the area to protect them from an attack on the airdrome. As well as flying a two-engine Whitley, he trained on an upgraded simulator of the Link Trainer. On the simulator, he learned how to use the new form of navigation called "Gee," a homing device which used radio frequencies to navigate in the same manner as shining flashlights from three different sources to a common point, the target. Before Gee, the only navigation method used by the RAF was "Dead Reckoning," which was to aim for the target and hope to find it with light from a "bomber's moon" (close to a full moon), and a compass as their guide. As the previous results indicated, it was a terribly inadequate system. Although Gee wasn't perfect, it brought a greater efficiency in locating the intended target.

Keeping in Touch with Home

In a short letter to Jean, he apologized for not writing. He promised to send her some pictures of the country, and he told her about his local transportation: "They issued us with a bicycle to run back and forth from our billets to the airdrome which we find to be a lot of fun." He complimented his sister Kae, saying she: "is a swell writer, I certainly have gotten my share of letters from her. I haven't written her near as many as I should have." He added a few comments about the kids: "So the small fry start to make trouble, eh? Again you have a growing family on your hands! And poor little Guy is beginning to resemble the uncle a bit, eh? Well, I hope his disposition is better than was D.C.'s when he was between 6 and 12 or so, if I can remember correctly."

From his letters, Donald seemed content with his present situation, but he was already looking to the next phase of his life. "Indeed, a lot of water has gone over since St. Thomas, and I hope that maybe this time next year I will have crossed the Atlantic going the other way <u>to stay</u>. It is swell here, but it just doesn't compare." He commented on the Dieppe raid: "Our little ole Canadians did OK in that Commando raid on France, eh? Cheers! The time is coming for Jerry." The high casualties of killed, wounded and POW's at Dieppe, however, indicated a very different result.

He praised his mother: "You stand congratulated! Four letters arrived in three days! It certainly was nice to hear from you that often." He was pleased to hear that the family had enjoyed their summer at Pog, but he was unhappy that his mother had not sent a recent photo - "are you allergic to a camera or what," - although he did mention that he had a "swell picture of you in my wallet." He asked her "to remind Jeanie that he would like a letter just to know she exists." For once, he told his mother that the weather was good, which meant he could fly. He asked for photos of the kids and told her he would send little cards for "the fry" in his next letter. His comment on the Russian front was a bit premature. "I think the change for Russia is due now and any day or week Jerry will be in hot water again." Unfortunately, that was not to be, as the Germans continued to advance on Stalingrad. Donald was confident things would soon change and issued a warning. "Now the nights are becoming longer, Jerry will also be receiving the odd calling card from us, and I think he will really moan." However, his desires were never far from his requests. "PS Try sending a <u>whole</u> canned hen. I hear they are super!"

In his next letter to his father, he asked: "Are you serious about having to close up the mill and not start logging for lack of labour? If that is so, keep a good eye on big brother." Donald did not want Bill to join the Air Force even though he had his pilot's license and was considering it. Donald hoped his father: "got up to Wye a couple of times. From what all the kids write they are fond of the place and that it is a marvelous set-up." And on another important topic of mutual interest: "As regards your query on promotion, one cannot tell. There is supposedly a ruling in the RCAF that six months after graduation you become a flight sergeant, a step up from pilot sergeant. Well, you know I am overdue, but I will wait for a couple of months and see what happens and if nothing, I will see what I can cook up." He thanked him for the Lauras but as he had not received any lately asked. "Have they stopped making them?" Donald referred to a new offer from his father: "Regards your letter of some time ago. You mentioned the deal after 21. You said it would be OK to smoke then, and the new deal was no liquor. Remember? It doesn't matter much, but I think I will get me a big black pipe. Not bad, eh? Write soon."

> <u>Sept 1 '42</u> Telegram – sans origin – MR WB PLAUNT EVERYTHING GOING FINE HOPE THINGS ARE SAME THERE LOVE DONALD PLAUNT

A week later he reminded his mother: "I just looked at my flying log book, and it is just about one year ago to the day that I had my first Air Force flip. Remember I had Kae's friend's brother. He added the first reference to a fourth grandchild: "Also another little stranger? Kae told me about it in her last letter. What are we going to call it this time?"

Jean penned a 16-page letter on July 29 in response to "Dunk's (her nickname for him) most enjoyable letter," and she pressed him for an honest answer:

> Try and be honest and answer this truthfully and don't forget to answer it. Are you flying in fights now or still training as you tell the family. Dad doesn't believe that. He says you must be in the thick of it since you've been there over three months. You might as well keep on telling him that you are training even if you aren't, but tell me the truth.

Chapter 8: A Return to Bonnie Scotland

Those three (grandchildren) are cute. They are creeping now and are they ever funny. Guy <u>creeps</u> on his hands one knee and one foot, and it looks comical. Andy doesn't use his hands or knees much, but scoots along in almost unexplainable fashion flat on his tummy."

I will send a box before I go to Wye. Just in case you haven't heard, chocolate bars and gum are now 6 cents and pop is 7. Ouch!

Jean told him that a Louis Armstrong concert she attended was: "marvellous, the music was <u>really smart</u>. Gosh, could they ever dish it <u>out.</u> I got their autographs and Bernard Flood said he'd send me a picture of the band and one of Louis Armstrong." She griped that she didn't go to the band's party[16] after the concert at the Nickel Range as she was concerned about her father's reaction. After a trip to see her grandparent's graves in the Bala area with her mother, Agnes and Kae, she was going to Wye soon: "Nothing like the excitement of

Jean Plaunt, Head Girl at Branksome Hall

---

16 There was a second Louis Armstrong concert in Sudbury on April 8th, 1952 in which the Plaunts were involved in hosting an after concert party. Armstrong and his band were invited back to Bill and Agnes Plaunt's home where my father (Mac Thomson) administered a shot of penicillin to the gravelly voiced singer who had complained of a sore throat. Their female singer commented that it was the first time she had ever been in a white person's home.

the backwoods, but it'll be livelier than Sudbury. Have fun kid. Lubb to all the kids. Write soon."

He responded quickly: "That was a darn fine letter. All the "gin" that was going on in the old home town." He knew she would be returning to school for her final year and predicted she would be head girl. She did become the head girl for Branksome Hall. For the following year, Donald saw their plans paralleling as he wanted her to attend the School of Nursing, and for himself: "Let's hope I will be home <u>then</u> to have a crack at university too. My, what a smart little sister I must have, up to my form with me." Then there was his usual lovelorn advice: "Little one, do not worry about our friend Con. The RCAF will do wonders for him. What is he enlisting as, or do you know? I agree with you that he just doesn't look any Clark Gable." And on their maturity or looks, he advised: "My God you must be living high. Looking older than me. I guess that is just how I used to be, I hope. Everybody over here thinks I am 25, and they won't believe I am any younger. Maybe I worry too much, eh?" As for his new base: "I can't say much for this one. One doesn't get any time off so you can get sick of it."

As to Jeanie's many questions, he replied: "I am afraid censorship will not permit me to tell you all you asked in your letter. I am on "heavies" (a type of two-engine bomber) and in a month or so I hope to fly the four-engine ones. They are pretty nice aircraft. I cannot tell you more." He mentioned he hadn't heard from Syd and Bill in over a month. And he ended with the usual request: "Write some more of the 16-pagers, only more often. Love Donald"

He continued writing that day to his parents: "Even the weather here has been quite nice although a trifle windy. I am getting used to it raining all the time now, so it doesn't bother me very much ... I hope the mill is running OK and that you are not having too much trouble with labour. No doubt conscription is causing the shortage to be quite acute. I guess that come September this war will finish and then you will be able to get all the labour you want." He told them he would be going to Edinburgh on leave as: "I liked the city very much in peacetime. Then my navigator

Chapter 8: A Return to Bonnie Scotland

and I will take a Lady Ryder[17] deal together for a week. They are darn good fun as a rule."

After receiving a box from his sister, Helen, he wrote: "Yesterday your very choice parcel arrived with a generous assortment. The Lauras were the type I like – hard centres, who told you?" He thanked her for a mirror and comb but then complained: "you do not write very often. However, I guess I can pardon you there as you are getting quite a formidable line-up of "gentlemen friends" in the services – Al, Higgie, Bill, etc. and so on, or need I rub it in?" And so often as he did with Jean, he opened up about his feelings about home: "I understand that you had a swell time at Fort William (now Thunder Bay). Good show! You may be sick of home, but I (the voice of experience) can tell you nothing is as bad as being homesick. Yah, I know I am a big boy now – but just the same!" He liked her food parcels: "I use your peanut butter and butter to make up lunches to take up flying for long trips. It is a darn nice rest from meat pasta, bully beef, etc."

He continued: "So the news goes around that again I am to become another uncle come Christmas, whady know? The picture of the three young ones is just about as cute as ever I have seen of them. I get a laugh out of it every time I have a look-see. Talking about a laugh – I haven't a picture, at least not a decent one, so come along little one." He boasted to Helen about Jean. "I received a sixteen (yes 16) page letter from the family infant and what she didn't tell only just hasn't happened in Canada in the last ten years." It seems the Scottish weather wasn't any better than the English: "Pretty awful flying today. And I spend a most enjoyable afternoon playing tag with the mountain goats on some of the peaks amid the clouds. Glorious fun, maybe not!" He ended: "Well, I can't say much about what goes on, so I may as well sign off. Thanks a million for the mirror and parcel my Love. As ever, Love Donald."

---

17 Although I could find no information on the Lady Ryder homes - she volunteered for Special Operations during the war and worked for many charities after the war - many people opened their homes for Allied servicemen for their leaves.

A week later he learned from his mother that all was well with the family, and she was happy that they were home from Pog preparing "to spend another blood-curdling winter in the frozen north." He commented on the new school year: "What makes me think of that is the fact that I, at last, got a letter away to my friend Mr. Hamilton (one of his favourite teachers at Ridley). I am somewhat sorry I hadn't written him before now." As to the other shipments: "I am receiving parcels okay except for the <u>shirts, shoes or gloves</u> as yet. The Sudbury Stars are still coming fine, and I received a pile of them today." He mentioned that he was going to write Grandma Hicks and his brother, Wee Willie, but "I find it very hard to write everyone as I must repeat myself to make any letter a decent length."

In starting his letter to his mother on September 23rd, he commented on his latest deliveries - a box each from Kae and Marion and a letter from Helen. He was enclosing birthday cards for the kids and stated that he would send Christmas cards later: "I didn't realize that Drew was so <u>old</u>! ... I hope Bill got the pipe I sent him OK for his birthday. I must be getting old as I fully intended to send Agnes a cable on their anniversary but forgot." He hoped his father would do well in golf as he "certainly gets a kick out of it." About the pending birth of the Thomson's second child, he asked: "How does Kae <u>know </u>it is going to be Katherine Anne? What if there is another tassel?" (a tassel was the family metaphor for a boy)

Going home became a more frequent topic: "Regards that Lancaster that flew to Canada.[18] They certainly are a lucky lot of fellows. The envy of the RCAF over here. You can see it isn't so far away, okay about 8 hours across the Atlantic." There were the usual topics: "Syd and Bill are on leave now, but I couldn't get away to spend any time with them. I hope to see them in three to four weeks. I expect that within four weeks when

---

18 See: http://www.bombercommandmuseum.ca/lanccanadian.html The Lancaster was flown to Canada to be a "pattern" for the building of many more Lancs by the Victory Aircraft Co. in Malton, Ontario. Lancasters began production by November, 1943.

I get my leave I will get another posting to a different type of aircraft. I have my fingers crossed for Lancasters. I will soon know."

Good News from the Russian Front

Donald raised the promotion issue when he learned that a fellow who couldn't pass a pilot's course, went into another trade, was commissioned, sent overseas, and now gives orders to <u>sergeant</u> pilots. It is a most amazing system." He was clearly frustrated; "Well, no longer do I care!" And finally, a comment on the Russian front after they had pushed the Germans back at Stalingrad: "Today the Russians are really showing up. Apparently, they have beaten Jerry back a mile. Let's hope that is the beginning of the end." [19]

On the 25th, he wrote to his father that his brother: "doesn't have the same pessimistic view you had of the logging camp. He tells me that you are getting some pretty nice stuff out of the last winter's logs and that you have some pretty good stuff to cut this fall. I guess by now you will be getting men from the farm so you will be able to fill up the camp. Bill tells me you have Fred Martel cooking so you won't have many worries there." And on the war: "The Russians seem to be giving Jerry just about all the medicine he can take. I wish we would open up the Second Front and do a bit in the winning of the war. It is a shame the Russians have to carry the whole weight of the fight." And a comment on the American industrial capability: "I see in tonight's paper where (American, Henry) Kaiser built a Liberty ship in 10 days. He certainly isn't fooling, the way he is slapping those scows together."

On October 6, he complained to his mother: "Say what is the hold up back there? The letters are certainly becoming few and far between ...

---

19 Although these words sound Churchillian, the prime minister did not deliver them until November 10 after the British victory in North Africa. "Now this is not the end. It is not even the beginning of the end, but it is, perhaps, the end of the beginning."

The parcels are arriving quite OK but still no sign of the clothes I need – <u>shoes</u>, <u>shirts</u>, <u>gloves</u> – now it is handkerchiefs, a dozen or so. Kae's shortbread was sure a treat. Also, the butter tart was OK. I guess you could send more of them. I certainly wish Grandma's donuts had arrived OK, but they were in bad shape." He added comments about a variety of topics:

> So Drew is coming into his own on the feeding, eh? What is the matter with the other two? I guess they will be walking and talking by now. I bet they certainly are cute. Do you know if Jimmy Hinds ever got my letter I wrote him several months ago? Tell him seeing the hockey season is coming around I expect him to do big things this season and I want to see his name in the headlines.
>
> There are some of the US Air Army Corps over here as you probably know, but they are being "babied" and have yet to prove themselves. They certainly talk a marvelous scoop. I must drop a line to Dad and thank him for the saving certificates. The family certainly must be collecting an awful hoard of them.
>
> No doubt you will remember me mentioning the name of Hugh Watlington, a boy from Bermuda, whom I used to chum around with at Ridley. Well, I was very glad to hear where he was awarded the Distinguished Flying Medal.

Bomber Assignment

As Donald finished his training at Kinloss, the moment arrived that he had been waiting for since he was chosen to be a pilot almost a year and a half ago. Would he finally get the plane to fly he wanted so badly? He was first rejected to be a fighter pilot, and now that he was on bombers,

Chapter 8: A Return to Bonnie Scotland

he had his heart set on the Lancaster. Donald's luck could go either way. Finally, his squadron leader called him for a briefing. Donald sat down, feeling nervous and excited, knowing full well that this was his moment. The squadron leader wasted no time. He smiled and gave Donald the word he wanted to hear, "You're on a Lanc!" Donald felt his heart rate double, but he kept his cool and just let the officer see one of his beaming smiles. At last, his biggest dream had been realized.

Donald's dream plane, The Lancaster

After the briefing, Donald quickly wrote to his father to tell him the exciting news. Donald was first going on leave, and when he returned, he would transfer to a Lancaster squadron. He expressed hope that along with being a captain of a Lancaster, he would get an upgrade in his personal status: "If and when my promotion comes through and I get a raise I am going to make a monthly allotment out of my pay for a war bond. I don't know what I spend it on, but I sure can't seem to hold on to much money as is. In the meantime, I am making myself popular around here giving away cigarettes, a thousand of which the Lumberman's Overseas Club sent. It certainly is a lucky break that I am on these Lancs. I believe that eventually most of our crew bombers will be of this type, and I am fortunate to be somewhere among the first group to fly them."

CHAPTER 9
From a Crowd of Strangers to a Tight-Knit Crew
(AUGUST 15 - DECEMBER 15)

"You can see the great melting pot this outfit is."

Donald's crew: Back Row (L to R) Joe Taylor, mid-upper gunner; Trevor Williams, flight engineer; Donald Plaunt, pilot; Jean-Louis Viau, bomb aimer. Front Row (L to R) Jock Lochrie, rear gunner; Ralph Frank, wireless operator. Missing: Alex Smith, navigator

On October 20, Donald took one last flight on the Whitley. By this point, he had recorded a total of 359 hours of flying since he first learned to fly in Goderich in September of 1941. Now, the moment he had been waiting for, to pilot a Lancaster. Despite his pride at being a Scot, he was glad to get away from Scotland because it was too hilly and the flying conditions were poor.

Donald and his crew headed to Swinderby, an RAF base located in Yorkshire County in north-east England. Established in 1940, the base was both home for several bomber squadrons, and as well, acted as a conversion unit to train aircrews to up-grade to four-engine bombers. To begin the conversion to the larger bomber, Donald's crew spent ten days flying on the Manchester, the two-engine precursor of the Lancaster.

Before his posting at Kinloss, Donald had been flying primarily as a solo pilot with an occasional instructor and navigator. At the Scottish base, he was flying bombers which required additional crew: a navigator, wireless operator, bomb aimer, flight engineer and one or two gunners. As in the selection of pilots, all aircrew went through a selection process that began at the Initial Training School followed by instruction in their specialty.

Crew Formation

Selecting a crew was a very sensitive and critical step in preparation for operations. Along with ensuring that each specialist was highly competent, the ability to work with, and trust each member was paramount as they faced life and death situations on every mission. The military understood the importance of creating these tight-knit groups or "band of brothers," as it was one of the most important criteria for the success of a military operation. Each member's commitment to this group is so strong that each was willing to die for one another. However, for that bond to gel, each team needed time to develop the *esprit du corps*.

Chapter 9: From a Crowd of Strangers to a Tight-Knit Crew

Donald travelled to Kinloss with the hopes he would be chosen to pilot a Lancaster. Despite wanting to be a fighter pilot, his character suited him more to be a bomber pilot and leader of a group of men. His family upbringing, his school leadership experience, and his personality combined to make him a natural as a captain of a bomber crew. The success of every operation depended on his capability to fly safely, smartly and with the self-assurance with which his crew would feel confident. Along with Donald's skills as a pilot, he possessed a natural charisma. He was easy going, humourous, generous and most importantly, beamed with self-confidence. He may have had misgivings about things that he expressed in his letters, but his peers only witnessed his strengths. Given his gregariousness and flying skills, he was a natural for that position. It didn't take long for his crew to warm up to the man they affectionately called their "Skipper."

There were different ways to select a crew of seven different specialists. On some bases, all aircrew were thrown together for a period of time before the teams developed. At Kinloss, they got to know each other in the mess, on training flights, or in the classroom, so there was ample opportunity to develop relationships that led to the formation of a crew by personal selection. The other method was to have teams chosen by an officer. However, given their limited knowledge of the crews, they would have a challenging time picking teams that worked well together. There was no doubt the former process was preferable, but sometimes the command had to appoint someone to fill a vacancy.

One hoped that the training process would weed out the incompetents, but there were often those who failed to live up to the expected standard or were troublesome as a team player. And even if you did form a crew of your choosing, there were unexplained reasons why a member was substituted. Donald had to face both these situations.

There was no mention in Donald's letters of how his crew was selected, but from his log book, it was apparent that a nucleus existed by mid-September at Kinloss. For the initial phase of training, they flew on a two-engine Whitley which required five members whom he listed: Ralph

Frank, Jock Lochrie, Jean-Louis Viau, Sergeant Jones and himself. Finally, Donald had a group to call his own. Though they appeared to be strangers at first, these five men would grow to be very close.

The Nissen hut provided a natural habitat to develop a camaraderie that was essential to the creation of a strong crew. The hut was a half-barrel-shaped structure of galvanized metal that provided their living accommodation. Along with beds, there was a coal stove to heat the non-insulated shelter. They worked and played together, as Donald described the scene with his crew to Jean:

Nissen Hut

Right now, my tail gunner, Jock, is batting away at the piano and every now and again is playing *Yours* which just about makes me weep.[20] Yes, in spite of its antiquity, it is still my favourite piece. One just doesn't hear any better over here. He was a pipe fitter and is quite a lot of fun and is half mad. But he is a good gunner and a nice chap. He is married and has a couple of children.

The rest of my crew is Canadian. My navigator is an ex-reporter and ex-officer of the Grenadier Guards of Montreal. I hang around with him. My wireless operator is a Jewish kid from Hamilton. He made his living as a horn player in an orchestra. He has us all in stitches all the time. One big laugh. His latest is that if we get shot down over Germany, we tell Jerry his name is Paddy O'Brian so they won't treat him too rough. My bomb

---

20 Hear Vera Lynn sing it as Donald may have heard it. https://www.youtube.com/watch?v=Tg3ZdMR3x_c

aimer is a French Canadian and was a civil servant and he, too, is a fine chappie. My crew is as mad as they come, so I am happy. All the boys are older than I, and all engaged or married, so I had better be careful of them, or there will be a few people pretty peeved at me. They are all hair brained though and go around calling me "Skipper" whenever they see me within ten blocks. But from that, you can see the great melting pot this outfit is. OK, did I forget to tell you who the captain was?"

He had found a synergistic team, with a proud and happy captain.

Donald demonstrated his sensitivity to the predicament of his wireless operator, Ralph Frank, as Jews were vulnerable if captured by the Germans. They joked about calling Frank "Paddy O'Brian," so the Germans wouldn't suspect he was Jewish. However, Donald had a better plan. Donald and Frank would exchange their ID tags before every departure. Although not all people with the name of Frank are Jewish, Donald's credentials of being a gentile could easily be verified.

Once settled on his new base, he wrote his mother stating his partiality over a recurring issue: "if it must be a choice between letters and parcels – I'll take the letters." He was not getting enough mail, so he reinforced his preference, despite his awareness that other factors were holding back her letters. He continued: "Because my wireless operator is Jewish we don't all fly for the next couple of days while he celebrates the New Year. He is a hang of a good kid as all of my crew are." Donald moved on to family concerns. He was already thinking of birthdays and Christmas which put him in a more positive frame of mind: "Mother – I hope you received your little birthday gift I picked up in Scotland. It certainly is hard to get anything that is suitable for you over here. I sent Dad's Christmas gift a week ago, so I hope he doesn't open it until Dec. 25th. I also sent home an RAF calendar that I thought might go nicely in the office. Take a look at that little airplane they give me to fly. I need not ask you if it isn't a dream. Its performance is much better than revealed. I am indeed fortunate to be flying the <u>world's</u> <u>best</u> bomber. So in spite of all my groans, there is something in the outfit I am happy about."

Despite his accolades for his crew, there was one weakness. He announced a change: "I fired my Canadian navigator the other day. Every time we went anywhere, we became lost. Being the captain, I would get the blame and then he pretty nearly put us in a critical hole. But with the "luck of the Plaunts," I managed to get home to a strange airdrome okay. I now have a Scotch lad, and he is very competent. I was certainly pleased to get off of the Whitley and doubly happy to get on the Lancaster."

The next letter to his mother was more nostalgic:

> Well, here I am in a bit different tempo than I beat on in that letter I wrote to you yesterday. It is Sunday evening, 9:00 pm to be exact, which makes it 3:00 pm in good old Sudbury. No doubt you were to church this morning. I was. It seems strange, but home seems strongest in my mind when I go there. I don't get there very often because I can't get away. The fellow that preached here today was of the Chinese race, from Formosa, but a <u>Japanese National</u>. He was very interesting and spoke very highly of the work the men like Mac's father have been doing in China.
>
> This afternoon I went to see William Powell and Hedy La Marr in *Crossroads*. I thought it was darn good. It seems funny, but here I look forward to my leave being over instead of the way it was at home. Tomorrow I am going to look up a couple of boys I was with at ITS in Toronto. Then Tues. or Wed., I expect to go down to see Syd Smith.
>
> Last night I was out and was dancing, but I don't enjoy it like I used to at home. However, I expect to be home in

Chapter 9: From a Crowd of Strangers to a Tight-Knit Crew

a year or so, so I guess I will get back in the groove. Well, Mom, I will sign off now and write some more on this tomorrow. Good Night.

In his next letter to her, he was in an upbeat mood:

Well, here I am back at work, and I think I like it here a lot better than <u>long</u> leaves. I enjoy short ones, but when they are too long, I don't enjoy it near so much. I certainly owe a lot of people apologies. When I got back, there was a real pile of mail, about eleven letters. The shoes arrived and are the cat's pyjamas. I hope you haven't worried too much about not getting the crepe soles as it really is of no consequence. Also, the shirts and gloves arrived. A1. Thanks a lot for them. I received a letter from Dad, Bill, Kae, Helen, Agnes and your three, so I have a good bit of news and don't feel so much like the forgotten man!

He promised to write Grandma Hicks, who had moved in with his Aunt Pearl in Brantford. In response to his father telling him he had bought more war bonds for him, he replied: "Where did I get all the war bonds? I didn't realize I was such a wealthy man!" The only news concerned his new crew: "Today I picked up two more fellows for my crew, a flight engineer and a mid-upper gunner. They are both English lads and seem to be very nice chaps indeed. Of course, I guess I have told you about this aircraft, so everything is hunky-dory." He told his mother that he had seen Syd who was hoping for a transfer to a new squadron. "Well my wireless operator is starting to blow his trumpet, so I guess I will have to sign off. I got to report for work in 15 minutes so *au revoir*."

His letter to "Dad (Champ)" on Nov. 9 was congratulatory and covered a variety of topics:

Well, yesterday your letter of Oct. 5 got to me, and you forgot to tell me that you won the golf championship. Come now, don't let modesty interfere with me getting the real news! If you win that much more, you should be allowed to keep the cup. Your admiring wife had to tell all about you hauling down all the laurels. I just saw in the paper, about Sept. 5, that the lumber industry is now considered a vital war industry in Canada. It certainly took them long enough to smarten up and to do so. Maybe because of that they may make it easier to procure men. Also, you can keep Big Brother at home where he will be of more use to the country. It wouldn't be too good if they took Mac at this time.

Talking of conscription. My poor heart nearly broke when I saw pictures of those poor hard working miners from Kirkland Lake and forced away from their homes to those awful nickel mines at only $1.00 an hour or so. What a laugh!

I see where the Yanks have landed in Africa[21], so I guess that kind of settles the question of whether we are going to go up through Italy or not. And when we do, I only hope we make a swath through that country that will make Sherman's march through Georgia look like a garden party.

That young Mahaffy is quite a "Guy." If he keeps on growing, he will soon be as big as his Mother. It seems funny that he should walk before Andy isn't it? I hope

---

21 Operation Torch was a combined invasion of American and British forces in French North Africa on Nov. 9, 1942

you get your Victory Loan over OK. No doubt you are still Chairman of the Finance Board. Best of Luck.

Mom told me you bought some piglets. Are they for Wye or Raphoe? Will you operate your trucks in the woods this winter or lay them up? No doubt you will do the latter and use horses.[22] Incidentally, how many teams do you have now?

Well, Dad, there is very little else I can write about so I guess I will have to close now. Write very soon Champ!

A Suspicious Sister

Jean's letter written on October 28 opened with "Dear Dunk, or should I say, Skipper?" She asked him some simple questions about his last leave: "Where did you go and who did you meet and what did you do. The truth please." She was suspicious he wasn't telling her everything, especially about his flying. She was pleased to hear he was flying a Lancaster. She reported that her school had raised $18,000 for the war effort, but did not specify for what. Her Toronto school was rehearsing for an air-raid and blackouts, suggesting there were fears of an aerial attack, although it is difficult to imagine from where. She filled him in on news of three Sudbury people who enlisted in the RCAF and mentioned the numerous military parades that were taking place in Toronto, which took two hours to pass by, along with a squadron flyover. She ended with; "Write soon and give my best to Paddy O'Brian."

Donald's response to Jean two weeks later contained much gossip, the usual reprimand, brotherly advice, news and requests:

---

22 See http://pogamasing.com/videos/ for how horses were used in the lumber industry at this time

> I am doing a not bad job of this, considering my Scotch air-gunner is working out on a chanter besides me ... I was to a little dance last night on the station. I had a pretty good time. But it didn't compare with the dances we used to go to at home ... There is a "red-hot" dice game here now, but I can spend my money quick enough without "the bones."

He continued: "Those pictures you sent me are a perfect example of amateur photography" - and a request to send more from Christmas time. She had told him of the death of their budgie: "but I guess it was time he had to go. That is the trouble with pets." He talked about her plans for next year and his own after he came home: "I am very sorry to hear that you won't be making School of Nursing next year but for gosh sakes make an effort at school this year and make a good showing, and then next year go back. You would think I am "shooting a line," as after all who am I to talk? But honestly, it will pay. If possible, when I go back, I am going to university, and it is going to be tough." He told her of the additions to his crew, adding: "Soon they will be enough to man a battleship." Of course, he couldn't help but end with an order: "Well Toots, I will ring down now and buzz off to the camp cinema but will write you again very shortly. Behave!!! ??"

The following day he wrote to his mother that he expected a visit from Wally Lawson and Bill Squire, his Ridley friend who travelled to Europe with him in 1939. Donald had received a letter from Montana where Squire had been training as a paratrooper: "He tells me that he is now a full-fledged para-commando and a sergeant as well. He also said that his command in the militia had just come through."

He hoped to get some Christmas shopping done soon but was finding it difficult to get to Lincoln to shop. Christmas was on his mind, and his stomach, so he added his order: "I don't know whether we will haul down much turkey for Christmas, but I figure we, if any, will get as much as possible. Can you procure it canned? How about those whole chickens? One

Chapter 9: From a Crowd of Strangers to a Tight-Knit Crew

might come in handy at Christmas or for New Year's." His thoughts about Christmas also included his favourite gathering of the year, the family party on January 1. "No doubt you will be entertaining again this New Year's. That is one grown-up do I did enjoy."

On his mother's birthday, he first wrote his father:

> I received a very nice letter from George Miller and he told me he was looking forward to a trip to Pog for a spot of hunting. He also tells me that you were going to plan the strategy of the war for the next six or eight months. If you planned this present North African campaign, you didn't do such a bad job. Things certainly do look much better now, and I hope they keep it up.
>
> I hope Sudbury District pulled up its sox and cleaned up its deficit in the Victory Loan, but as you say, it is a tricky district because of its population. It should be different as those people should be the ones to "shell" out. I guess they will never learn. It seems strange tho', as I have told you my wireless operator is a Jew and my bomb aimer is French, and they are both darn good types. I don't find that either of them clings to their racial characteristics. So as you always said, there are good and bad in every nation.
>
> This may seem strange, but the people I don't like too well are the English. Individually, they are OK, but they do not trust each other, particularly labour and capital. You may think it bad, but here they are always at one another. This business of strikes is another thing that amazes me. Labourers, men and women, who never did receive any pay at all before the war, now are drawing fair wages, and working not too bad hours, earning twice

to five times as much as the forces. They can go on strike or bellyache; but if a soldier, sailor or airman does the same, he could be shot. I think that privilege should be extended to the strikers as well!!

Well, as you probably know by my last letter, I am very lucky and now have the privilege of the best bombing aircraft in existence. When you see a piece of designing and workmanship like that, it is when you have to admire the English!

The food we get on this station rates on par with prison fare and I will be glad when I have moved again. It won't be far from here, but it can't come too soon.

Well, Dad, I hope you have the same "do" at New Years. It certainly is a grand party. Hope you have a good time at Christmas. You should with all the kids running around. Write soon.

He then sent a telegram to his mother:

> Date unknown - Telegram - MRS WB PLAUNT DEAR MOTHER MANY HAPPY RETURNS LOVE DONALD

Along with the cable from London, he wrote to wish her Happy Birthday. He warned her that her: "Christmas gift will probably be there around Jan. 31st as I know what I want, but I have to wait until I get to a decent spot to get it. I hope Dad got his package and is holding off until Christmas. I hope they are not too small, but they were the last brace (pipe stands) Dunhill's had at their factory in London." The weather was typical for this time of year and was interfering with their flying and he

Chapter 9: From a Crowd of Strangers to a Tight-Knit Crew

wished for: "a good Canadian fall. No doubt you have had quite a bit of snow to date and will have plenty more before Christmas." Syd had been to see him for a couple of days out of his leave of six days; then he was off to London to visit relatives. Syd told Donald that because Bill was in a Canadian squadron, he was given a commission, while he and Donald didn't get it because they were still RAF.

Donald sent "some silverware" for the kids' birthdays but admitted it wasn't something the boys would appreciate so he "would like that the boys had something they could appreciate more when they get older (like a gun!)." He was grateful for the scarf his mother had sent and then added his order:

> Say, send me some Indian relish will you, please. Frankie (Ralph Franks) got some the other day, and it sure tasted swell. A good idea would be to buy a whole box of butter and each time you or the kids send a box, insert a can in every box. I like it because we have a lot of toast we make ourselves, and we need plenty of butter... We, "the boys," bought a little hot plate so often our room is transformed into a veritable kitchen. It is certainly handy as the food is rather wretched on the station.

He ended: "Write soon and often. Merry Christmas."

Write Soon and Often

> Nov. 21 '42 Telegram — Lincoln - MRS WB PLAUNT SEND CHRISTMAS BOX FOR THREE YEAR GIRL FOR MY GUNNER LOVE DONALD PLAUNT

In a letter to his father the following day, Donald failed to explain why they had not been hearing from him. It was the first time his parents noted the lack of mail and hopefully made him realize his letters weren't getting through as quickly. "Your package of 1,000 cigs got here this morning, so I guess I will be making myself popular handing them out." He explained a telegram he had sent to his mother: "I cabled Mom for a box for a 3-year-old girl. As you know, toys, good candy, etc. are at a premium in this country and my Scottish tail gunner has a little 3-year-old girl, so I thought it would be nice if I could have some stuff sent over for her before Christmas." He indicated a difficulty regarding his mother: "She certainly is presenting me with quite a problem for something for Christmas. I guess the kids and she will understand if things arrive a bit late." Then he was off to do some Link training with his flight engineer who acted as a second pilot since the position of co-pilot no longer existed on the Lancaster. "Write soon and often and thanks for the cigs. Merry Christmas and remember, have a Happy New Year's Day."

The following day Donald wrote his father to thank him for the box of Lauras that came that day. He decided to give this box to his tail gunner's daughter. His crew wasn't happy, but Donald's concern for Jock's child overruled their appeal. His justification: "She can have them for Christmas, and it will be much better than any she would get in England. I also hope Mom gets a box away in time as that should be very nice for her Christmas. I guess there are a lot in her position in this country and at home."

Chapter 9: From a Crowd of Strangers to a Tight-Knit Crew

Watershed Month

If there was a turning point in the Second World War, it was November 1942, when the Allies finally stopped losing major battles, or as Churchill stated, "… it was the end of the beginning." The Russians had encircled the Germans in Stalingrad, the Americans had defeated the Japanese at Guadalcanal, the Allies had landed in Morocco, and Montgomery had defeated Rommel at El Alamein. After the French Vichy government refused to comply with the Allies request to hand over their Navy of 17 ships, the Allies sunk the total fleet stationed in Toulon. Donald commented: "That certainly was a real funny set-up in the French Navy! Poor old France is really in a nasty spot now, no Army and now no Navy. I guess the French will be cheering a little more for our side now, and not so many of them will be going to the Russian front to fight for Adolph." By the end of 1942, the tide of war shifted to the Allies and Churchill commented: "Before El Alamein, we never had a victory. After El Alamein, we never had a defeat." Unfortunately, it took another year and a half to finish it.

Donald updated his father on his friends: "Syd was up here just the other day, and he is keeping fit. He was going to see the "Cowboy of the Sky," our nickname for glamour pants "Spitfire" Lane. That is right; we are jealous of him. Flying the fighter is fun and not the work and responsibility we get in these darn bombers. But mark me, they are magnificent aircraft in spite of that." He asked about the lumber camp operations and enquired why Mitch Hepburn had resigned as premier of Ontario. "Well, I flew quite a bit today, and I am rather tired, so I must close now. Write often."

In his letter to his mother the following day, he thanked her for the three letters that arrived yesterday. He told her about sending the box of Lauras to his tail gunner's daughter, justifying it by: "I kind of feel sorry for the little kid; her Dad won't be home for Christmas and no doubt she will miss him." He commented on the quality of entertainment he heard on the BBC: "I just finished hearing a program featuring Edward

Robinson. He certainly was darn funny. Now there is a program on featuring Kae Francis, Carole Landis, and Martha Ray. Those programs are really tops in comparison with the BBC's usual stuff. If you thought the CBC was "corny" you should just get a sniff at this corporation." He added some more comment to the sinking of the French fleet: "I don't know just what went on, but it sure seemed strange, and it is a crime that <u>we</u> didn't get hold of some of those nice big battleships, etc., and it would have helped a lot." He tried to send a photo of a Lancaster but was overruled by an intelligence officer. Naturally, there was his detailed mail order list:

> Maybe this is too late but if you would like to pick me up a <u>classy</u> dressing gown, perhaps RAF colours or something like that, with a monogrammed pocket and a good pair of slippers. My old plaid job I got when I first went to Ridley that Mr. Hamilton and I purchased is shot. However, if you can't get a pretty good one, better you should wait until I return. It is the only private spot of clothes I can wear when on duty. I suggest you get Bill to pick it out as his taste isn't too bad in those affairs. Also don't get slippers like you sent before, send ones like Dad has. OK? Well, I guess if I go on I will ask you too much so I will close for now. Write me soon and try to insert *Acta Ridleiana* in my next parcel."

That same day he wrote to Kae: "Well Lord Haw Haw[23] has assured us that the Jerries are winning the war although I am inclined to think slightly different. What stuff you can pick up on the radio over here?" He told her that he had to fly in fog and haze that day but that they returned and "everything is hunky-dory." He commented on what he was hearing about her family: "They told me that Drew is whipping around like a wooden soldier on his two pins and making a pest of himself. They tell

---

23 British traitor who broadcasted German propaganda to Britain.

Chapter 9: From a Crowd of Strangers to a Tight-Knit Crew

me he is going to have a little brother! True or false?" He thanked her for the last parcel, and especially, a folder of photos but "conspicuous by their absence were pics of you, Helen and Jean. How about that." And he concluded: "Well, Kae. I must go and bathe, shave and hit the hay. Write soon and give me all the dope on R.M. Jr." Donald had a preference for naming children after their fathers, which in this case would be Robert MacKay.

> <u>Dec. 4 '42</u> – sans origin –telegram – MRS WB PLAUNT - RECEIVED SHOES THANKS EVERYTHING FINE LOVE DONALD PLAUNT

In his letter of Dec. 7, he told his mother that he had been a beneficiary of a "smashing" parcel from her friend, Mrs. Humphreys, and from the Service and Cheer organization. He mentioned he would write to thank them and added, "I have been very lucky as you and the kids have been right on the ball, so I sure cannot complain." After another parcel arrived he revealed his concerns for children in Great Britain and what he missed about Christmas: "Today Guy's packet of Lauras arrived, so now I will give the box I received from Dad to Jock's little girl. I am afraid I wired a bit late concerning a Christmas box for Jock's daughter. I imagine that little kid has never seen a city light up at night, it seems so unfair in a way don't you think? Talking about lights, no doubt there will be a curtailment at home, but I bet the Christmas lights will be lovely. One doesn't appreciate those things 100% unless you don't have them."

His displeasure with his young sister returned. "What kind of friend is she, one letter since August that is pretty awful." But he wouldn't let his displeasure stop him from sending her a Christmas present. He asked his mother to explain to Helen and Jean that their Christmas gifts will probably arrive in February as "I know what I want, and I <u>am</u> going to get it."

On the first anniversary of Pearl Harbour, Donald wrote his father about the photos in the Sudbury Star: "You sure were good looking in all of those pictures that were in the paper with regards to your chairmanship of the Victory Loan. I never did hear whether your district made their goal or not." Another thank you for the Sweet Caps: "I am going to distribute them among my crew for Christmas."

WB Plaunt receiving a recognition award for work on War Bonds from the Minister of Defence, Hon. James Ralston

Inaugural Flight

On December 8, Donald and his crew took their first flight on a Lancaster. They flew routine circuits to familiarize themselves with their new aircraft. He said nothing of the trip to his father, but covered a series of topics that were a good summary of his present mood and future plans:

> I just finished a pretty nice supper, and you can be sure that I didn't get it at the mess hall. I guess it would knock your eye out to see yours truly munching on some

canned meat, bread, some cheese and enjoying it. I certainly could go for a lumberjack meal right now, not to mention at home.

Well, regardless of how black I paint the picture, I am still my delicate little self, all 210 of me. I guess I will have to thank your Laura Secord's for that. But we sure are glad to get them. I see where the girl who works there keeps a count on them. I bet she must think I am an awful glutton.

I would love to have my little car over here. It really would make things better. Then again there would be the matter of petrol. The irony of it all is I carry over 1,000 gallons every time I take off and burn a terrific amount in the air. But I guess the car business is something that will come with *la victoire*. Soon as I get the dough, I am going to buy me a nice big Cadillac convertible coupe. Modest tastes what? But seriously, next to home I miss not having a car and every time, I think of the good times I had with the Chevy, and there were lots. I am thankful that you bought it for me.

Well, Pop, now I must think of my baptism to vice. Next time I go to London, I am going to Dunhill's and buy me a nice pipe for June 1st. Remember our deal. No smoking and drinking until 1/6/43 and no drinking after that. I miss a lot of wild times by not, but I do not regret it. Most of the fellows after arguing with me all evening to have a few, admit that they wish they didn't booze. Sounds funny at this ripe age but in most cases, it is a safety valve. I guess your money is well spent, as I have yet to hit a number of the flying personnel that doesn't drink. So see, you saved me from a drunkard's existence.

If I am not flying tomorrow evening, I hope to go into [cut out] and see Jack Benny in *Believe it or Not*. I have seen it before but if I remember it was *par excellence* so I will see it again. It is a good laugh. I wrote and told Mom I want a dressing gown and slippers. If she is getting them for me, you keep an eye on her and see that she gets them pretty *pukka*. I must close now and whip off a couple more letters to others, then take a bath, shave, and go to bed. Write often Dad.

Donald and his crew spent ten days in December perfecting their skills in flying the Lancaster. Their training consisted of circuits, local flying, and night flights combined with bombing practice. The next step would be an assignment to a squadron for the last stage of training before heading into action.

In his last letter from Swinderby on Dec. 12, he wrote to his mother: "Well, here it is the twelfth month and wee Sandy's birthday. It certainly is different here at this time of year than it is at home. Why the grass is still green and little sign of snow. It still is pretty foggy, though, but the condition is improving as a rule." He mentioned he had received three letters from her dated Oct. 23 to Nov. 11 and was puzzled why the letters were arriving so irregularly. He expressed his appreciation of hearing from his friend Crossie Clark's mother and his Aunt Pearl. He continued:

Tomorrow I expect to go to town and get my Oxfords out of hock, that is, I have just had their third pair of soles put on them. They wore really well – were Churches. I now have that pair you sent from Blanchford's. So as you see I am OK regarding shoes. Talking of clothes what goes

Chapter 9: From a Crowd of Strangers to a Tight-Knit Crew

on regarding the dressing gown? If anything, make it a good one.

I have just heard Lord Haw Haw, and I agree he is rightly named, he is just one big laugh. It is a shame there are Englishmen like him. It is too bad that young fellow is like that, as his father is quite a big shot and an esteemed statesman.

So glad to hear the Victory Loan went over so well, but did Sudbury District, Dad's part, reach its goal? So one of the men at Raphoe thought the soup was thin! That burns me up. If he were forced to eat what most people have to eat here, he would more than howl. It is substantial enough, as a rule, but nothing particularly tasty."

So at last Andrew is walking, eh? He seems to be a lot slower than Guy in those sort of things. I bet he will talk the first of the two. So how you do like Rev. Combs? At least you said you liked his sermon. It is funny what you said about the way you felt when you were at church. I think I wrote and told you about the same thing here. When I get a chance to, I go, but that only occurs when I am on leave. Must be off. Write often.

As November 1942 had been a turnaround month in the war, it was also a pivotal time for Donald. He was flying the aircraft he wanted with a compatible crew, and by his admission, he was "happy." Donald's comments indicated that he liked his Lanc crew immensely, especially Jock Lochrie and Ralph Frank (Paddy O'Brian). With a newly formed "family" overseas, letters from him stopped coming as regularly. There were still times when they would go to the pub, leaving Donald time to write home. He was now comfortable living his life as a pilot of an aircraft he wanted to fly. As Christmas approached, Donald certainly felt less lonely and more useful, than when he had arrived nine months ago. With their training almost completed, Donald's crew were now posted to an RAF squadron for an orientation period before beginning operations. The Allies strength was increasing, and as Harris initiated his strategic bombing offensive, Donald would be involved.

CHAPTER 10

Christmas Overseas

(DECEMBER 15, 1942 - FEBRUARY 5, 1943)

"Well here it is Christmas, and although it isn't anything like the good time we have at home, it isn't too bad considering."

Squadron 97, Straits Settlements

Donald and his crew reported to 97 (*Straits Settlements*) *Squadron*, part of 5 Group in Bomber Command, based in Woodhall Spa, Lincolnshire, in north-east England. The RAF had established a tradition of naming a squadron after a donor in appreciation for funds donated for the purchase of aircraft. The Straits Settlements, a group of British territories on the Malay Peninsula in south-east Asia, had given funds in 1941 for the purchase of Manchester bombers. As mentioned earlier, Avro redesigned and upgraded the Manchester to a four-engine aircraft and gave it a new name - the Lancaster. Squadron 97 was initially a Manchester Squadron and was one of the first to upgrade to the Lancaster when it came into operation in March 1942. Donald and his crew were posted here on December 15, 1942, and would train for six additional weeks before beginning operations.

In writing to his mother on Dec. 17, Donald apologized that he had not written to her for ten days because he was "very busy and on the move." In her previous letter, she had mentioned that his brother Bill and his wife Agnes were expecting another child. "I am indeed glad to hear of the arrival next June of W.B. III, eh!" He was pleased with a parcel from Marie Cook of Sudbury High School, and letters from Mrs. Humphreys and Mrs. Prince, two of her friends. He described his surroundings: "Right now it is 6:00 pm and I am in pajamas and bathrobe sitting in my room writing. I just got the fire started and am quite comfortable, and I am going to get caught up on my mail. The weather is bad, and the squadron has a stand-down, so rather than go to town I shall have a pleasant evening "at home."

Unable to fly, Donald had time to plan his upcoming eight-day leave: "Christmas doesn't have the same significance over here for me. People don't enjoy it so much, and then again, I haven't seen any snow yet. Just fog and rain." In response to his mother's question about being a 1st or 2nd pilot, he answered: "I am the 1st pilot and captain, and still I am an almighty sergeant. Not bad, eh?"

> Dec. 18 '42 — telegram - sans origin — W PLAUNT LEAVE ON MONDAY FOR CHRISTMAS WITH BILL MAY YOU ALL HAVE A VERY HAPPY ONE ALSO THE PARTY ON NEW YEAR'S IS AS GOOD AS EVER LOVE DONALD PLAUNT

Christmas with Bill, but Syd Missing

On December 25th, Donald wrote a joint letter to his parents: "Well, here it is Christmas, and although it isn't anything like the good time we have at home, it isn't too bad considering. As you probably know by my cable of Dec. 22 I am on Bill Lane's base for my leave. Unfortunately, I couldn't have Christmas dinner with him as he is now a pilot officer and I don't belong! It is too bad, but it can't be helped! In spite of everything else there seems to be no shortage of liquor and everyone, excluding me of course, is quite inebriated, "ye olde English spirit," you know."

Chapter 10: Christmas Overseas

Despite the uplifting spirit that Christmas usually brings, the two Sudbury friends were feeling disheartened. They had just learned that Syd was reported missing over France on December 9 on a return raid from Turin, Italy. "Christmas for Bill and I is somewhat dampened due to Syd's absence. However, we are quite confident he will turn up as a prisoner or make a clean escape from France as it isn't too tough a proposition."

Bill Lane with Donald, Christmas 1942

He completed the letter the next day: "Well, as you see I didn't get this letter finished Christmas Day. Bill turned up and we went to town and had a very nice tea at a home in Darlington. Bill didn't feel too well so he hit the hay early and I went to the dance on the station without him. The more I see of this place with the Canadian squadron, the more envious I am of Bill. He has the "swellest" bunch of fellows imaginable here - all pilots and the same types – so it is much nicer." Donald was curious to know: "How is Katherine Anne Jr. coming along these days? No doubt the older gaffers had quite a time at Christmas or, at least you would have had quite a time with them. Well, *Pater et Mater*, Willie is champing at the bit so I must awa'. Goodbye now."

When he arrived back at the base on Dec. 30, he was astounded at what Santa had brought him. Donald was quick to tell his mother of his good fortune:

> Well, you can imagine the mighty pleasant finale to an excellent leave when I arrived back here and found twenty-one letters waiting for me and four parcels. It certainly was swell, quite a variation of persons too. Of course, from you and Dad, Kae, Jean. Mrs. A. C. Edwards,

a lovely letter indeed, Mr. Hamilton of Ridley and my young friends as well, Jim Hinds and Gordon O'Reilly. I received a super camera from Helen, Bill and Agnes so tomorrow I will take some snaps and will send them some <u>immediately</u>, if not sooner! A swell box from Kae including sox, braces (scarce as hen's teeth over here) and a real sweater. A big sweater arrived from Jean, for my birthday 1941, remember?

I am writing this under the greatest of difficulty. You remember, I told you that my wireless op was a horn player, well my flight engineer turns up with a guitar, so they are both hammering away. Well, tomorrow night is New Year's Eve, and I am thinking of the swell times we had on that date and on Jan. 1st, I hope you have the usual time "at home." I will celebrate my New Year's at 6 am Greenwich time and at 12 pm Sudbury time, the same time as you will.

You asked about Mason Hargreaves of London. Yes, I knew him real well and roomed with him at Kinloss. The snaps I sent you were his and were in his kit when he was shot down. It was the same time I had to force land at [cut out]. It is not my idea to report that sort of thing in a letter but seeing you knew his mother.

Well, Mom, I have been flying tonight, and it is getting quite late so I must say goodnight for now as I could use a bit of shut-eye. Write soon and often. I will answer your letters next time I write. A very, very, Happy, and again I say, Victorious New Year Mother.

Chapter 10: Christmas Overseas

PS Perhaps you have noticed I have given my squadron number. I just found out it was OK to disclose it. I thought I couldn't send it before because of security reasons.

Hogmanay

On New Year's Day he wrote three letters, the first one to his father:

> Well, aren't I the lucky guy? I get two letters from you on the same day, one of Nov. 19 and one Dec. 1st, as well as 22 other letters. The news, as you said, is improving although there was a short lull in December. I guess from here in is the big show.
>
> That was a darn good show you and Sudbury District put up on the Victory Loan. I knew that Canada as a whole had gone over the top but I hadn't heard about the nickel district. Will you be mixed up in the next one in May, maybe?
>
> Where are the five mills you have operating? With all those running, you should be coining the money no![24] I hope your labour troubles are somewhat relieved by now. I hope the horses were OK that Bill bought, but as a rule, the ones you got in the past from Renfrew were always tops. Bill wrote me from there, and he says that Renfrew is really booming because of the mine nearby.

---

24 No was the correct answer as businesses were restricted by the War Time Profits Act and profits were heavily taxed.

It certainly is unfortunate about Syd, but I wasn't too surprised to hear about it as both Bill Lane and I felt that it was coming sooner or later. It was no reflection on Syd's ability of course, but it was "just one of those feelings." However, we are still hopeful that he may be kicking around France or is a prisoner of war. It is too bad it happened when it did as he was due to go onto a Stirling almost immediately. He was flying a Wellington.

I hope you will excuse any black smudges you may see on this, but I have just been stoking up the little coal stove. These English have yet to hear of central heating it seems, so for any heat, we must keep the fire cracking.

We had our first snowfall in the last couple of days but now it has turned to slush and is most uncomfortable and most disappointing. In spite of the inclement and damp weather we get here, I have been rather fortunate and have had no more than the sniffles. I guess this is largely due to the ultraviolet treatment (for health benefits) we get four times weekly.

I got a card from Major Page today and from LAC Morris. Mr. Morris is getting his commission as an intelligence officer, and it certainly is just about time! Also, he is getting married again. I can hardly get over that! You know he has a boy 12 at Ridley too.

PS I like that photo of you, the cabinet members, and the soldier from Dieppe! Also, send me one of your new portraits, please!

Chapter 10: Christmas Overseas

Christening of Kathie Anne Thomson by her grandfather Rev. Andrew Thomson, with her parents, Kae and Mac Thomson. Rev. Thomson had recently returned from China

His second letter was to his sister Kae:

> I certainly am a rat for not having written to welcome Katherine Anne Jr. But again, I use the same old alibi of not enough time. So I am staying in for "Hogmanay" or, in other words, New Year's Eve, to get caught up in my correspondence. Imagine staying in on such a night? However, I can't complain as I had a few days leave at Christmas which I spent with Bill Lane and had a super time.
>
> Now I must thank you for the lovely Christmas box with the card I enclose. It really did seem like Christmas receiving all the things wrapped up so lovely. I am very glad to hear about Mac's Dad getting his honourary degree as Doctor of Divinity; he certainly had it coming to him.
>
> Boy am I ashamed of my eldest nephew. Imagine, at his age, wolfing, then letting a little girl like Sandra blacken

Write Soon and Often

his eye. I bet Mug Mahaffy wouldn't let a dame do that to him!

Yes, indeed, hurrah for the USA. Again they are winning the war for us. But even so, they are doing a good job. But I do get sick of hearing their fantastic claims of how many Focke-Wulfs they bang down each trip. I hope the RAF calendars get through to you okay. They are all I could find – I almost forgot, the shortbread is super and I certainly am enjoying it. I have a new navigator, a PO Alex Smith from B. C. A real nice chap but I am still skipper of the kite!

Well, Kae, I will close now, thanking you, Mac and all your family for the Christmas parcel and will remember your excellent advice to fly low and slow and to throttle back going around the corners.

Love to all and a Happy New Year.

Also in this envelope was a list of goods Kae sent in the "Fall 42" – Christie biscuits, 2x cheese, meatballs, steak and onions, pickles, chicken, chocolate sauce, nine gum bars, date bread, tea and sugar Sent Oct. 17'42 received Nov. 17,'42.

His third letter to Jean evoked his charming eloquence and youthful absurdity:

Bonne Annee, ma petite soeur! In other words, it is New Year's Eve and I am celebrating it by writing to you and a few other chosen ones. Boy, would I like to get in the necking and mugging you will tonight, and here I am cooped up 1,000,000 miles from nowhere, with only O'Brian (Ralph Frank) to kiss in bringing in the year of

Chapter 10: Christmas Overseas

the great and final victory. On taking a good look at him, I've changed my mind and will kiss no one.

Ah me, I guess it is an awful life, but to me, it will be OK just as long as it keeps on going for a while. My dear, dear little sister, thank you a million for your swell sweater and scarf. The sweater fits fine, and the scarf is just the thing. Also, the array and assortment of the candies were just something I dream about, so consider yourself a pretty good box packer-upper.

Aha, so your loved one is off to the wars, my beauty, no doubt he received Lovelace's old line about "I could not love thee dear so much, Loved I not honour more?" [25] Boy, see what education does for one! What is the wee lad going to be, pilot!

Your marks are not too bad, but I <u>know</u> you can do better in your languages and English. Come on now smarten up! Your zoology is damn good. Don't ever let me hear you talk silly about joining the WAAF's. If I thought a sister of mine was in that I would desert and join the Chinese Air Force. You smarten up and go on to Public Health Nursing and really do something <u>worthwhile</u> ... So promise me, Jeannie, don't ever talk of the WAAF's again.

So you want me as Air Marshall eh? You don't like your little brother as a plain old Sergeant Pilot. Well, well! However, without saying too much, I figure that there may be a change coming very soon! But say nothing. No doubt you know Bill Lane is a pilot officer, which is OK.

---

25 Richard Lovelace: from *Lucasta, going to the Wars*

I spent Christmas with him and had a darn good time. I understand that Mike Kennedy is becoming a bomb aimer and will soon be coming over. No doubt you heard about Syd. There certainly aren't many of our class left, and there is only one other fellow and me in operations in the whole class, so that is pretty tough.

Well, my Luv, it is time I had a wee bit to eat so I will toast me a few slices of "national bread," and go to it. Write soon and often and send lots of pictures. Thanks again for your sweater, scarf and parcel.

On New Year's Day, his heart was back home when he wrote to his mother at GMT 2100 hrs: "Well I don't really know what to say as I only wrote to you a couple of days ago and little has happened since then. However, look at the date and Greenwich Mean Time and you will see it is 3:00 pm Sudbury time and I can see the mighty line up at the door of 340 Laura Ave. Boy, that is a real party! Then a nice New Year's dinner at 8:00 pm with perhaps Mr. Collins. Am I correct? Well, I guess there is no harm in dreaming."

> Jan. 8 '43 –TELEGRAM - sans origin –WB PLAUNT - EVERYTHING FINE HOW IS KAE JUNIOR LOVE DONALD PLAUNT

On the envelope of a letter to his mother on January 10 there was an unusual Army PO stamp. There was no flying time recorded in his log book, but he partially explained his absence was due to being forced down at a strange base: "I am afraid I have not written to you for a week that I have been away from my airdrome. Bless this English weather! Plenty of sleet and snow is floating around, and it is damp out." On his return to Woodhall Spa he wrote to his father:

Chapter 10: Christmas Overseas

Well, this certainly is the strangest bit of weather I have ever seen in January. I am in my hut with just my uniform on and no fire, and it is Jan. 12. No doubt you think I am just too lazy to build a fire.

I hope your business is progressing quite favourably. No doubt Junior (brother, Bill) is having a time running things and will have relieved you of a lot more work than he used to. If all these reports I hear about you, chairman of this and that, off to the Conservative convention at Winnipeg are true, then he will have been running things.

How is Katherine Anne? Have you got her all spoiled like you had the other three – four – my, that score is certainly adding up. I am somewhat peeved at you for not having sent me your new portrait. All the letters I get from those at home tell me how good looking you have become, but still I get no picture to prove it to me.

Well, it looks like our big show is coming up and that the Jerries are going to get some "shelter huddling" hours in. It is only this bad weather that has been saving them from a lot of worries. As you probably heard, there has been a Canadian Bomber Group formed. In a way, I am not sorry I am on this English squadron as the Canadians ones have inferior aircraft.

His letter to his mother included the names of people who had written him and a few who had sent boxes of Lauras including Mrs. Smith and Captain Barnes of the Copper Cliff Highlanders. Naturally, he would write a note of thanks. He told her a bit more about his visit with Bill Lane during the weather-bound layover. "He is quite fit and is enjoying his life as an officer. I certainly am glad he got that break. It will be much better for his health too, as you know he never was too strong. So where he is, he gets much better quarters, food, etc. Talking of food, Mrs. Reed's butter tarts arrived here in swell condition and did they ever hit the spot. We are certainly enjoying them very much." He apologized for not sending anything home on Marion's birthday in December but he: "nearly went crazy trying to get Jeannie a pair of RAF wings for hers. They were all I could think of so again I was stuck." He finished: "The weather is so mild I haven't worn my great coat yet. I haven't even got my (sergeant) stripes sewn on to it, and I have been a sergeant for almost one year. It was Jan. 16 wasn't it? You have the date on your gold wings. Well, Mother, I am afraid I must close."

Although Donald had written Kae on Hogmanay to thank her for his Christmas gifts, now he responded to her letter and sent some photos that were extracted by the sensor. This letter looked more like a hunk of Swiss cheese as there were so many words cut out:

> A bit late, but seeing as this is the first I have written you in '43 so Happy New Year!
>
> I have here your letter of Nov. 10 which I have just received. Of course, you have made no mention of the new addition to the Thomson family that helps complete its domestic happiness! Wow, what a line! Anyway, how be she? I am anxiously awaiting a picture of her.
>
> Shooting a line about what type of aircraft you think I am on. Well, [cut out] I've enclosed a little picture of one. I guess you get lots of pictures at home of them, but I thought this was a good one so [cut-out] I was on [cut-out] for quite a while [large cut-out] Then for a while I was on [cut- out] then-! My big ambition now is to become [cut-out], but I am afraid it is my job to [three

Chapter 10: Christmas Overseas

lines cut- out] (Oh what a line!!) However, you asked for it.

Well, Kae, I must close now and write umpteen other letters. Goodbye for now.

> <u>Jan 18 '43</u> — Boston Lincoln —telegram W PLAUNT EVERYTHING FINE WRITING TOMORROW LOVE DONALD PLAUNT

Syd's Escape

On January 20, Donald wrote to his mother with the news they all had been waiting and hoping for: " the grand news is that Syd is OK. I hope that is what Dad's cable meant. Funny, I knew all along that he wasn't dead and that he would get out okay. However, it certainly is grand news, and I am glad for the family. Smitty has a lot coming to him. By that I mean he has worked hard and saved a lot of money to put himself through university as a dentist, and it wouldn't be fair if he misses it. I hope he gets his commission and a decoration out of it!"

Syd's escape was similar to Allied aircrew shot down in occupied France. He landed in a rural area and was fortunate to find an Allied-friendly family. They shuttled him to a larger home where he stayed with the female owner (her husband was a German POW) for a few days. Her daughter came to get Syd and took him to Paris where they would not arouse any suspicion. They had contacted the French underground who arranged for his escape. Syd's handlers smuggled him through France and Spain to Gibraltar. He never knew the names of his benefactors, including the lady who first contacted the underground,[26] as the Gestapo had ways to force captives to reveal their names. Once back in London, he was debriefed on his escape and ordered to say nothing, even to his closest friends.

Donald's letter to his father acknowledged his cable regarding Syd. "If I weren't half expecting that news I would be unable to believe it." He phoned the third Musketeer, Bill Lane, and left a message "so I guess he should know the glad tidings." He was pleased to hear that their Christmas and the New Year's party had gone well. But, he warned him; "I bet your Christmas season next will be a lot more hectic when the wee ones begin to know the score." Donald also mentioned that a family friend Bob Fee "turned up OK as a prisoner of war in Eye-tie land."

Later, Mildred Plaunt received an unexpected note from Bill Lane.

> Don has probably told you of our Christmas together. It certainly was nice to be together for a week, and we had a very good time. Shortly after Christmas, he had to land up near me because of bad weather and we spent a couple more nights together when I wasn't flying.
>
> Syd's little "do" must have caused a lot of anxiety at home but it was a low price to pay for the latest news of him. He should be back here very shortly.
>
> Don and I are quite a distance apart now, but anytime he gets leave I can meet him in London almost every night. My brother Gordon is down the line just a few miles and we've been skating together a couple of times.

---

26 Syd was the first of many airmen Mariette Grellet helped escape. Syd met her many years after the war. See *Lifting the Silence* by Syd Smith.

Chapter 10: Christmas Overseas

Thanks again for the Christmas card and please give my regards to the family.

Sincerely Bill Lane

Donald informed his mother that her Christmas parcel for Jock Lochrie's daughter had arrived. Donald reported that Jock went "crazy, so I guess the little girl should be pretty happy about it." She even named the doll in the box, "Plaunty" after her Santa Claus. He acknowledged a pair of knitted gloves from his grandmother and promised to send some photos.

One topic that was becoming more frequent in his letters was the loss of people that he knew. He heard that a friend, Ken Templeton, was getting leave to go home, because his brother, Phillip, who Donald had trained with in Yorkshire, was killed. He hadn't forgotten his newest niece. "By all means, get K.A. that knife and fork and also I insist that Kae take the money for the bracelet for the kids from the $21 a month if you or the government can spare it. I hoped they could get something like that. I will send more if needed." He added that Kae had: "sent me a clipping of the newcomer's hair and it certainly is nice. However, if you all are even just hoping for curls, just remember her two uncles and then give up all hope." He added: "I liked that picture of you in the Sudbury Star very much indeed. I am glad there is someone in the family to keep pace with my photogenic *pater*. Well, Mother, I must close now and will write soon again."

Was it a New Year's resolution or just coincidence, but this was the fifth letter he was now promising to write soon, instead of requesting letters to be written to him "soon and often."

His newest form of transportation reminded him of what he was missing as he told his father:

> I have me a bicycle that I had to pay an awful price to get hold of and now whipping back and forth on it. I would

certainly like to have the little car here. Keep it in good shape because I feel I am going to be using it a lot before I turn it in for my Cadillac convertible.

I bet you have Mom's new dog spoiled already and have him eating off of the silver service et cetera like you had the rest of them doing.

Say, how do you like things concerning the war? They certainly aren't going half bad. First, the Russians are going to town, then the Libyan campaign and lastly, the humble efforts of the RAF over Berlin and other spots. I guess there are no complaints, eh?

Well, as you have noticed I have been a sergeant over a year now, and I am beginning to get used to it. As a matter of fact, I am almost starting to enjoy it, as it isn't half so bad as it seems.

Well, Dad, I will write again soon.

As he wrote to his mother at 22:00 hours on January 27 he could: "hear the bombers coming back. As you can guess, yours truly did not participate this evening." What he could not tell her was that his squadron had flown in a mission of 157 bombers to Lorient, a German submarine base on the coast of France. He was late writing her because he had been to hear a Forces' concert which he found "pretty awful." He listed some letters he had received from her: two from Brantford, where she was visiting her mother and sister Pearl. As well, others came from Helen, Agnes, two from Jeannie Ross. He expressed his pleasure of the prospect of a new robe his mother was sending him; "Wasn't it just Christmas?" But then hoped she "didn't forget the slippers as well." He wanted more details about Syd's escape: "I wish you would let me know more about Syd. All

Chapter 10: Christmas Overseas

I know is that Dad cabled me he was safe in Gibraltar. We always kidded one another that if we found ourselves in Jerryland, we would try to put it over, and Syd did."

He turned to answer her "questionnaire," as he put it: "Yes, I received the big Christmas cake, and it certainly was a hit. The boys hadn't seen anything quite as good or as rich since Adam was an infant. I thought I had cabled you about it and also the crepe-soled shoes. Both pairs of shoes arrived safe, and they are certainly very nice and fit very well. I also received about 10 Christmas boxes in 3 or 4 days." In answer to her question about their lodgings, he replied: "Dispersed – it means everything is spread all over to fool any attempts to bomb it. We live in small Nissen huts about 1 ½ miles from the airdrome."

He asked about his cousin, Burleigh Plaunt, who had enlisted in the army and offered this opinion. "I am so glad now that I wasn't drafted." And on his favourite topic: "Well, Mom I guess I should mention about the can of chicken you sent me in the last box. It was super duper. The best I have had yet. I hope you did get a good supply. The mints are delicious, and I am looking forward to more, and you can take a standing order for the Indian relish. It lasted about 5 seconds. Also, how about some green olives, maybe." Donald commented on the Casablanca Conference between the two major Allies: "Our friends Churchill and Roosevelt sure get around don't you think? That sure was a surprise to me, and I guess Adolph too! Well, we are going to have a little snack, so I will close now. Good-night."

Training heavy bomber pilots took the longest time, and consequently, was the most expensive training position for the military. Only the American Air Force trained their bomber pilots longer, some taking approximately 600 hours. Since enlisting on May 23, 1941, Donald had spent a year and a half preparing for his combat role. As it was such a substantial investment in time and money, a lot would be riding on his shoulders. Surprisingly, the heavy responsibility and stress of training for going into battle were rarely reflected in his letters, other than his complaints.

By February 3, Donald and his crew had completed their training with a final check for beam flying, bombing, air firing and a cross-country run. Their last training flight was a three-hour simulated night trip called a "Command Bulls Eye" on February 6th. They had to navigate to a specified location, such as a large town or city, and respond to what the simulated German defence system would throw at them. They were now ready to join the squadron in operations. In total, Donald had recorded 415 hours of flying, including 56 hours on single-engine aircraft, and over 350 hours of dual and four-engine aircraft.

> <u>Feb. 5 '43</u> —telegram - SANS ORIGIN W B PLAUNT IN GOOD HEALTH LOVE. DONALD PLAUNT

A few days later, on February 7, Donald piloted his first mission. From then on, there was the added stress of operations: the challenge of flying in a bomber stream of several hundred aircraft, search lights, night fighters and anti-aircraft batteries. Could he live up to the *Acta* description of him as a goalie at Ridley: "His forecast reads getting hotter all the time, but not much change in temperament?"

CHAPTER 11

Missions

(FEBRUARY 7 - MARCH 12, 1943)

They lived it up like there was no tomorrow. That was the Air Force style. Sadly, for two of them, there would be no tomorrow.

New Strategy for Bomber Command

The War Cabinet issued a directive in February 1942, "to destroy the enemy morale." This new approach was a significant change for Bomber Command. At the start of the war, Bomber Command was only used to drop propaganda leaflets over Germany. From there, its focus shifted to bombing oil production facilities, isolated industries and laying sea mines. The latest directive decreed that Bomber Command would now drop bombs on industries in the centre of cities for the purpose of destroying the will of the civilian population. To implement this aggressive strategy, the command's new leader "Bomber" Harris introduced new tactics in flying formation, navigation technology, bombing tactics and verification. Implementation required further training for aircrews to coordinate these innovations with the new aircraft.

The massive number of bombers would now fly in a pattern called a "bomber stream." All aircraft would fly together at the same speed and altitude towards a common target. The formation worked as a defensive tactic as well. If they kept together as a unit, only strays were easy to attack by night-fighters, much like a herd of caribou against a pack of wolves. The danger of collision while flying in massive numbers would be offset by the advantage of overwhelming the night fighter radar so that more planes could reach the target area. The RAF limited the operation to one primary objective a night, with one or two secondary attacks just to keep the German defences dispersed. The new formation was launched on the city of Cologne with an impressive 1,000 bomber raid on May 30, 1942, and continued for a longer period to include other industrial cities such as Essen, Hamburg and Berlin.

Some new inventions bolstered this strategy. An innovative navigation system, called Oboe, used radio beams emitted from stations in Britain aimed at the target area to guide the bombers with greater accuracy. Unfortunately, only a few planes could use Oboe at one time. As a result, aircraft called "pathfinders," positioned at the vanguard of the bomber stream, marked the target area with flares. Air-raids to destinations close to Britain could use Oboe but targets further away were limited because of the curvature of the earth. A new onboard radar system called H2S[27] was developed to overcome this shortcoming, which meant distance did not limit bombing targets. Also, to ensure accountability and to check for accuracy, all bombers were outfitted with cameras to take photos of their bombing runs. Finally, the introduction of a combined bomb load of blast and incendiary bombs was employed: blast bombs to open up buildings and incendiaries to burn them. It was a very nasty business.

Despite these innovations, the success of the new approach was limited by Germany's improved defenses. Radar stations positioned at intervals along the Dutch coast notified night fighters and anti-aircraft

---

27 H2S was an early form of on-board radar that could identify some landmarks. The origin of its name was due to the reaction of the creators' boss to the new technology. When shown the new radar , he said, "It stinks." Consequently, the innovation was named after the stinky gas hydrogen sulfide (H2S) When the technology was ready, they took it to Churchill and he asked them why the unusual name. They were afraid to tell him the truth so they replied: "Home Sweet Home." H2S was superior to Oboe because it had no distance limits as it was an on-board system (*Most Secret War* by E.V. Jones) Thanks to Fred St. Lawrence for the loan of the book.

batteries of impending attacks. Although British Intelligence developed counter techniques to jam German radar to minimize detection, it was impossible to slip through unnoticed. The defensive advantage came by approaching their target in a bomber stream in a short period to overwhelm the German defences. However, returning aircraft, especially if damaged, often fell out of formation and were vulnerable. Despite all the improvements to Bomber Command, there were still losses, between one and ten percent per raid. As long as the destruction of German cities and industries outweighed the RAF losses, the War Cabinet carried on with the Harris strategy.

Preparing for Missions

The preparation for each mission involved a standard routine for everyone participating in the night's raid.[28] Bomber Command HQ chose the target and distributed the details of the attack to all squadrons. The mission had to be meticulously coordinated to ensure safety and effectiveness. Shortly after lunch, everyone involved in the mission met in their briefing room to hear the particulars from the wing commander. Central command distributed intelligence reports regarding German defences along with a weather report. The wing commander disclosed the flare colours to mark the bombing target, and finally, announced the take-off times and the rendezvous area to bring the vast armada together.[29]

---

28 I derived much of the routine from Doug Harvey's *"Boys, Bombs and Brussels Sprouts"*. Thanks to Kathie Thomas for this source.

29 See this site for an excellent series on Bomber Command photos that includes every aspect of a bombing raid. https://en.wikipedia.org/wiki/RAF_Bomber_Command_aircrew_of_World_War_II#/media/File:Join_an_Air_Crew-_in_the_RAF_Art.IWMPST14630.jpg

Loading bombs in a Lancaster

After the full squadron meeting, the specialists, such as the navigators and wireless operators, gathered in their respective groups to clarify their roles. As well, the ground crews checked the mechanics of each aircraft and loaded their planes with the night's payload. The most common load consisted of one 4,000-pound impact bomb plus 12 or so SBC (small bomb containers) comprised of a couple of hundred four-pound incendiary bombs. Along with the high explosives, each bomber carried 1,000 gallons of fuel or more, depending on the distance, plus over 100 gallons of oil and fluids for the miles of hydraulic lines, and 14,000 rounds of ammunition. Everyone knew, that if shells hit your plane in a vulnerable spot, it could mean instant death.

Then the most difficult time of all - the long wait before take-off. Each man and crew found ways to pass the time, either alone or out on the playing field, to distract their minds from the night's mission. Every man had his personal superstitions and routines, each done to ensure a safe return. Just before the mission departure, crews gathered in the mess for the traditional bacon and eggs dinner.

Take Off

One can only imagine how it felt to be in one of those heavy bombers at the start of an operation. First, ground crews started their engines and once every plane was warmed up, the 10 or 12 aircraft from each squadron took off in single file. It would take an hour or so to climb through the clouds with the heavy load of gasoline, ammunition, and bombs to the 20,000-foot level. If it was still daylight and clear, they could see the amassed fleet of bombers surrounding them. On most of Donald's missions, there were approximately 350 airplanes, creating a stream fifty or so miles long by 3 to 5 miles wide. As he glanced out his window, no matter what direction, there were bombers, like a school of fish, all heading to a common destination. As the sun set in the west, the sky would darken and slowly the hundreds of bombers would fade into darkness. At this point, each pilot was now dependent on his instruments and his ability to "fly blind." Using the Lancaster's advanced technology, a skilled navigator and Donald's own above average night vision, he had a good chance to reach the target. It would not be a quiet or smooth flight as the four Rolls-Royce Merlin engines roared and vibrated, like a pack of Harley-Davidson motorcycles passing through a mountain tunnel, and as well, caused internal vibration, intensified by the air turbulence from planes in front.

As the bomber stream crossed over the French or Dutch border, the eyes of the various crew members kept a vigilant lookout for night fighters or friendly aircraft that might stray too close. The rear gunner, in his 270-degree Perspex bubble, had the best chance of seeing an approaching fighter who preferred to attack from behind. From the front of the aircraft, and below the pilot, the bomb aimer had a wide-angle view of the forward area through his bubble window. The mid-upper gunner had a 360-degree view from the top. Each crew member flew with the confidence and expectation that each man was on duty every moment of the trip.

Despite Bomber Command's innovations, the German air defensive system had also improved. German radar was now more sophisticated and was able to detect the intruders and alert their night fighters and anti-aircraft gunners faster. Hitler's move to expand the night-fighters made their squadrons a fierce and deadly opponent. As well, the Germans had positioned batteries of searchlights around the main cities, so that several beams of lights would focus on a single aircraft and their anti-aircraft batteries would fire on the illuminated airplane. These blinding lights could paralyze a pilot unless he responded immediately to take evasive action which meant diving straight down to the earth in a corkscrew motion until the aircraft was free from the lights and out of the view of the German flak guns. With the diving aircraft plunging straight to earth, the pilot then had to use brute strength to pull the plane out of the dive.

First Raids

A new directive from the British War Cabinet on January 15, 1943, ordered Bomber Command to hit German submarine bases for the next month along the French coast to reduce the submarine threat in the Atlantic. Donald's crew took part in the attacks on Lorient in three of their first four missions, beginning on February 5. The submarine base was a difficult target because it was located within a French city on the southern Brittany coast. Unfortunately, the submarine pens were so well fortified with reinforced concrete that there was little damage inflicted. However, the bombing destroyed much of the town, killing innocent French citizens in every raid. The justification for bombing beyond the submarine pens was to destroy the transportation routes that brought in supplies to the base and thus reduce the submarines opportunity of quickly returning to the Atlantic.

Debriefing

Bomber crews were accountable for each mission they flew. As well as carrying a camera to record photos of their bombing run, they were expected to file a report of the night's raid to the senior officer of their squadron. After they had returned from the mission, all crews gathered in the briefing room to report on their flight. The reports covered a variety of topics such as the location of the target area where they dropped their bombs; the number and types of fires they observed; weather conditions in the bombing area; any mechanical or damage they encountered and observations regarding enemy defences. For example, Donald's report on their first mission read: "Primary target Lorient successfully bombed. Thin cloud. Identified southern point of town visually. Saw at least 15 good fires burning. Bombs released and seen to burst in the midst of burning area. One very yellow fire seen." They were awarded an "OE" (operational excellence) award for precise aiming, an excellent showing for their first at bat. However, this recognition and a second one they received a few nights later (see below) did not seem to mean much to Donald as he described them as "token" awards. The effectiveness of each attack would be later assessed by combining photo analysis, the Red Cross reports and intelligence reports from spies.

Operational Excellence award for accuracy

In his first letter home to his father on February 11, there was no indication that Donald was now flying on operations. However, his father would not have forgotten his remark that he was going to be taking a few trips before his next leave:

> Syd came up here a couple of days ago and this evening he has returned to London with the promise that he will come back before he finally leaves for home. I received the box for Jock's little girl and apparently she is the *belle* of the town.
>
> Thanks an awful lot for putting that $500 war bond away as it sure looks like it is going to be mine. Incidentally, it is a good thing you had that little offer on, not because I am inclined to drink, but it is as common to see boys

Chapter 11: Missions

and girls 16+ in this country drinking beer and stuff as it is for them to drink coke at home. [piece ripped out] Drinking is a national institution here.

No doubt you would like some recent pictures of the Lanes (Bill and brother Carleton). I am sending home a few prints of shots that were in the paper with Syd. My leave is coming up, and I expect to spend it in London with Syd and Bill. Mike should be over here very soon. It will be funny to see <u>him</u> again. Maybe we will have a real Sudbury reunion in London!

His letter to his mother a few days later was not much different from his father's. He told her that Syd would take a few items of his stuff home, including a radio and his watch that needed repairing. He had a half a dozen letters to answer, but the lack of parcels was bothering him: "I am getting near the end of my rope regarding supplies as there hasn't been a parcel here for over a week. I am looking forward to Indian relish and apple jelly if you have lots."

To his brother Bill, he opened with a wisecrack:

Well, long time no hear from! What's the matter, working too hard keeping the wolf from the door?

I trust Agnes and wee Sandy are in the best of health and enjoying life. I had a letter from Agnes a couple of weeks ago, and she says that everything is OK. They tell me my little sister and father had a bit of a run-in over the smoking matter. Maybe I am old fashioned, but I am so darn sick of seeing women smoking and drinking I can appreciate Dad's sentiments. Pop tells me they are knocking hang out of your bankroll on the old income tax.

Well, things over here are still stooging[30] along the same. I saw Syd a couple of days last week and then for some excitement I am going on leave in a week so that I will whirl down to London way.

Well, I got me up at 4:30 pm today. Sleeping off a sore bottom after 10 hours on a trip to Italy. The Italians put up a much better show than usual. I can see why I had a bit of trouble the other night, and they had to change all four engines at 2,000 pounds each or about $40,000, so it ain't hay.

> Feb 21 '43 — telegram - sans origin (London) WB PLAUNT ON LEAVE WITH BILL AND SYD HAVING A GRAND TIME LOVE DONALD PLAUNT

A Sudbury Reunion

For the three Sudbury buddies, a chance to spend a leave together was a long awaited and highly anticipated occasion. All three were now piloting combat aircraft: Bill a Spitfire, Donald a Lancaster and Syd a Wellington. But most of all, it would be a time to celebrate Syd's safe return from his ordeal and to hear about his harrowing escape through France and Spain. Donald wrote very little about their reunion, but fortunately, Bill wrote Donald's parents with a few details, and I was able to get a fuller account from Syd, both in an interview and through his book. As Syd wrote:

---

30 British slang for paying someone to do an unpleasant job.

Chapter 11: Missions

We agreed to meet at the *Chez Moi* pub near Piccadilly Circus. We hoped the other member of the Four Musketeers, Mike Kennedy, now a bomb aimer in a Lancaster with 101 Squadron could have joined us, but he couldn't swing a leave. As I walked into the pub, I spotted Don and Bill leaning against the bar, their hands flailing in lively conversation. I ducked around, snuck up behind, and tapped them on their shoulders both at once. They swung around in unison, their faces blazing with that familiar vitality. We exchanged first-rate Canadian bear hugs, which turned a few heads in our direction, then bellied up and caught the bartender's attention. Don looked as hale and hearty as ever, his jet-black shock, now a crew cut and the tallest standing crew cut you'd ever see while Bill had cut some handsome lines in an already good-looking face. It was great to see them.

"Smitty, I always knew you'd turn up!" Don said beaming. "Remember how we all kidded one another that if we ever found ourselves in Jerryland, we'd put it over on them? Well, you did!"

They carried on for the rest of the evening swapping stories although Syd could not tell them much about his escape from Paris to Gibraltar. Air Force personnel were aware of the requirement to keep those matters secret to protect the escape route, especially the men and women who risked their lives to escort them to Gibraltar. They joked about the rivalry between fighter and bomber squadrons and Donald loved to tease Bill, calling him "Glamour Pants Spitfire Lane" and the "Cowboy of the Skies." But as Syd recounted, both he and Don were concerned about Bill's desire for revenge for the killing of his older brother Carleton and they were worried he would push himself too far.

Donald and Syd in Trafalgar Square, London

While on their leave in London, the three comrades stayed at the Regent Palace Hotel, a landmark hotel that resembled our own Royal York and according to Syd, Donald picked up the tab. Syd told me they even took a taxi from one side of Piccadilly Circus to their hotel "just for the hell of it." Donald, of course, resumed his customary deep water baths, walked around the room in monogrammed bathrobes, but did not have a drop of booze or a smoke. He still planned to collect from the deal with his father. Breakfast was ordered each morning from room service, and bellhops and waiters were well rewarded, courtesy of their generous benefactor. They lived it up like there was no tomorrow: that was the Air Force style. Sadly, for two of them, there would be no tomorrow.

There were lots of things to do in London. They spent time seeing the town, checking into the Crackers Club, a favourite RAF club to play darts, shuffleboard and to admire the "local colour," as Syd told me. They took

Chapter 11: Missions

in a long-running play *Flare Path* by Terrance Rattigan, about anxious RAF wives awaiting their husbands from bombing missions. And they visited their former Sudbury Y program director Joe Barratt who worked at the London YMCA to check out if there were any Sudbury boys in London and to swap stories about their earlier times together in Sudbury.

Later, Bill Lane wrote the Plaunts and described their memorable London leave:

> Don and Syd and I spent seven days in London about six weeks ago, and I think it was the best leave any of us have ever had. We had two double rooms in the Regent Palace Hotel, and we lived like millionaires till we had spent all our money. There was another lad with us, Dusty Miller, from London Ontario and between the 4 of us we easily spent over 100 pounds but it was sure worth it. We managed to find a couple of steaks and ate about four chop suey meals. Don still won't take a drink although we did spike his grapefruit one night to see what he'd do. I've never seen anyone drink so much orange and grapefruit in all my life. He got great delight in kicking my hat whenever he could get his hands on it. One day he and Dusty kicked it down four floors of the hotel and out into Piccadilly. One night they even filled it full of beer so you can imagine what it looks like now. I think he derived even greater delight out of mauling Syd's hat because it was newer than mine. Don was about to go up for his interviews for his commission and probably had his first one completed.

Donald's description of the London reunion to his parents was brief:

> I am afraid that this letter is going to be about half as it should be, but I have only a little while to spare. I have

> just returned from leave which I spent with Syd and Bill in London. As you expect, I had a wonderful time. We were hoping that Mike would have turned up, but I guess he was just on his way at the [cut out]. I am sending some negatives home with Syd and also a few good pics of Lancasters and a couple of token awards to my crew. You can save me the latter two if you will as they will make a swell souvenir for me.

Back to Work

After a week's leave, Donald and Bill headed back to their respective bases: Bill to his Spitfire No. 403 Squadron at Kenley, 40 kilometres due south of London, and Donald back to Woodhall Spa in Lincolnshire, 200 kilometres north-east of London. Syd was given an extended leave of three months to return to Canada. On March 3, Donald wrote a note to his parents before the raid on Hamburg:

> Glad to hear everything is well at home and that the children are all OK. I received a series of snaps of Guy, your little dog, and Sandy. Are they both as cute as a "mouse's ear." Guy looks the mischief maker he is. Today I received my robe and slippers, and they are marvelous. Thanks a million both to you and Dad.
>
> So you like what is happening to the U-boats, eh?[31] I guess they have it coming to them.
>
> Well, Mom as I said we are awful busy, so I must sign off now and go to tea. Thanks again for everything.

---

31 The Allies were now sinking double the 1942 monthly average.

Chapter 11: Missions

The following evening he wrote his mother a longer letter:

> Well, here is an evening off, so I shall settle down and write a few letters. Jeannie has certainly staged quite a comeback and from her, I have received quite a few letters lately. My robe and slippers are swell. As a matter of fact, guess what I am wearing now.
>
> I had a smashing time with Bill and Syd on my leave and went through a mint of money. Breakfast in bed and all that sort of stuff, but as we have only a week out of seven I rather enjoy taking things easy. I ran into hundreds of people I knew in London and enjoyed that. I met a couple of my ex-instructors from Brantford whom I told what I thought of the way they handled things in that class of ours.
>
> Bill wrote and asked me what the new member of the family should be called DC (Donald Cameron) or WB (William Bell). Well, Mom, there is nothing I would like better than to have it called DC unless it is WB, after Dad and Bill himself. You know how proud I was of Sandy so, I told him to call it W B III. Don't you think that is the real McCoy? Anyway, it wouldn't be fair to name the poor thing after the sergeant in the family.
>
> "Bender," the squadron mutt, has just come into my room and is now reclining graciously on my rain cape. He seems to hang around me quite a bit, so you see you aren't the only one with a dog. I will send you a snap of Bender, so you must send me one of your pup.

> I am sorry you are not getting all of my mail, and I feel I am not receiving all you are sending me, but I guess we will just have to do with what we are getting and hope for more. Today I received the *Reader's Digest* for February. Thanks, again. I will write again soon. Now I must write to Dad and Jean etc. You could try to get Syd to bring my gray suit over. It isn't important if he can't.

After all his grumbling about the lack of mail from his little sister, Jeannie finally wrote him an eight-page letter. Just after New Year's, she wrote: "This holiday has been very quiet except for the three tigers tearing the place down. Guy Jr. is the worst. He races up and down stairs and never stays still. The young one (Kathie) is as cute as they come and she has a terrific mop of hair."

Jean told him that their father had found out she was smoking, and he warned her of the consequences if she didn't quit. She was most upset because he was a bit hypocritical as he "smokes, drinks and swears." Although Donald would listen, he was more on his father's side since he witnessed the effects of too much drinking among young people in Britain. Jean was ecstatic to hear about Syd's safe arrival as it: "was the best news for months ... I was so darn glad I ran around letting yells out of me all night. I started a letter to him then and finished it Saturday morning." She also told Donald of a dream: "That night I dreamed I had joined up, and then I went home to tell Dad and was I ever scared. If the war isn't over by the time I get my Matric (grade 13), I'm going to sign up and the heck with university until after the war."

She acknowledged Donald's thoughtfulness for her 18th birthday: "Your flowers came on Monday, January 25th, which was hardly late at all (her birthday was on the 22nd). Daffodils, iris and roses and they are gorgeous. I was so surprised and thrilled ... it was such a surprise since I didn't expect them after I had the cable from you. Well, Bug-eye, there is absolutely no news. Write soon." His refrain was catching on.

Chapter 11: Missions

Donald's amusing banter and big-brotherliness came into play in his response to Jean:

> A million and one apologies. I am afraid I boobed badly when I said you weren't such a hot writer. In the last two or three days, letters number 3, 4 and 5 converged on me in rapid succession and believe me, it was very nice hearing from you again. Until letter #4 arrived, I was saving up all my miserableness etc. to write to you regarding your joining the services. I am glad for your sake and the family's that you decided the smart thing to do is carry on at university and become a Public Health Nurse ... it is your real duty to all concerned to carry on there. So, I beg of you to take my advice, and do as Father wants you to.
>
> Boy, can I ever shoot a line – but I mean it! Also – congrats on giving up smoking. I really go for that. Just like Pop ain't I. Oh, Oh – I just hit in the part of your letter where you are talking about joining up, and I am seeing things.
>
> Quit being smart about "my old age" but a half dozen people in London guessed I was at least 24. So !!! Well, here are a few snaps.
>
> So you have yourself in hot water over the dance. That's what happens when you go running around falling in love! I hope it straightens itself out OK. I bet the Branksome ring is pretty smart – so hold on to it and don't go giving it away. I still have your little pin, and I never make a trip without wearing it – a real charm it is too! No doubt Campbell is quite the dashing young

airman. You can tell him he owes me a letter. So the little lad has a case on Marilyn, eh? Remember your little love affair with him when you were in Andy Grieve's class?

I would just love to see you in that play that you are in – No doubt you make Garbo look a pika (a small rodent), with your feet, of course, not the acting. So a friend of yours from Missouri decided she is going to be my girlfriend, eh? Well, if she is as cute as a girl I once took out from St. Louis Mo. I have no objections. Ask her what she is going to do about it.

The hair, for God sake, leave it long. That is another reason I don't like the female services, they all have short hair, so leave yours long. How about that picture you were going to send to me?

I saw some pretty good shows when I was in London including *Casablanca*. There was a black singer in it I really liked. We (Bill, Syd and a Dusty Miller from London) had a swell time – most of the time the boys were a bit high. Even Syd – but don't tell him I told you so. He is going to see you when he gets back. He is now a pilot officer. Poor me – the only duck in the bunch.

Now I come to a part of your letter where you are really talking sense – university! Listen, even I have a complex about the lack of education, and I am not just kidding. I am going back to school, if possible. Now I am afraid I must close, so keep on writing and send me lots of pics and some of you.

Chapter 11: Missions

> Love to you, Plunkett [32]

Jean received this letter after Donald was reported missing.

After the operation to Hamburg on March 4th he wrote his father:

> I received a box of Lauras from you and Helen sent in January. I also have Mr. Parker's pipe tobacco which I shall keep until June 1st. Well, it does look like our big air offensive is due to open up. I think we shall give them quite a thrashing.
>
> I had a swell time with Bill and Syd. I guess you know that Syd and Bill are both pilot officers. Maybe I should apply, eh? I will when I get 3 or 4 more trips. I shouldn't have much trouble then.
>
> Well, Dad, there is little news. Oh yes – I have one of your business pads, and I am keeping sort of a diary so maybe you will get a real line on what is happening some day. Well, *au revoir*.

Donald's reference to "our big air offensive" referred to Harris' bombing offensive which began on March 5 to the Ruhr Valley with Essen at its heart. The Ruhr was close to Britain, and had a multitude of important industrial targets, most notably the Krupp industries. Other centres, like Berlin, needed to wait until the fall as Bomber Command needed longer nights for the increased distances. Although the heart of the spring offensive centred on the Ruhr Valley, Nuremberg, Stuttgart and Munich were also included, and Donald and his crew were involved.

---

32 Given she was acting this reference is possibly referring to Canada's armed forces' entertainers Mert and Al Plunkett, part of The Dumbells.

Although his father suspected his son was flying missions, Donald also dropped a subtle hint. Before a raid on Munich on March 9 Donald told him: "Sorry I haven't written before now, but as you can imagine, we have been kept quite busy. There is very little news I can tell you about." There was, however, some news that Donald wanted to share: "Here's a bit of a secret. The Group Captain asked me if I was keen on a commission – so he said he would try and gin it as soon as possible. It takes so long for them to come through. That Dad is definitely on the QT, so please don't mention it to anyone, "as there is many a slip between cup and lip."

From Donald's log book, it appears he did not return to his base after the Munich raid on March 9 as he landed at an RAF base in Tangmere, just east of Portsmouth, on the south coast. The following morning, he flew to his base and conducted a night flying test for 35 minutes on a different Lancaster. That night he flew a mission to Stuttgart and reported a troubled starboard engine but was still able to drop bombs on their target and return to his base.

The March 9 letter to his father would be his last letter home. Telling his father about his pending commission would have pleased Donald immeasurably, but would have meant little to his worried father as the family had received the telegram notifying them of Donald's "missing" status on Sunday morning, March 14, many days before the news of his promotion arrived home.

CHAPTER 12

"Regret to Inform You..."

(MARCH 14, 1943)

"I am afraid that this letter is going to be about half as it should be, but I have only a little while to spare."

Donald returned to Woodhall Spa on March 1, after his leave with Bill and Syd. He was still in a euphoric state of mind from the week with his buddies. His comment to his father was brief: "I had a swell time with Bill and Syd." Now getting back to business was his priority. Bomber Command was currently focusing on the Bomber Harris "main offensive" strategy, beginning with the Ruhr Valley on March 5th. All of Donald's missions would now be to German cities. Of his first five missions before his leave, only one was a German target. The next six would only be to German cities (Essen-2, Stuttgart, Munich, Hamburg and Nuremberg). The German cities were daunting objectives because of their formidable and effective defences.

Crew Subs

Replacements began to occur in Donald's crew. What was most noticeable was the substitution of two crew members that had been with Donald since their formation in early September. They were also the two that he talked most about and whom he seemed to have particularly enjoyed. On Donald's first flight after his London leave, Jock Lochrie did not participate. Then, on the following mission to Essen, Lochrie returned, but it would be his last mission with Donald as he dropped out permanently due to illness. For the last four flights, Lochrie was replaced by Sergeant Baggs for one flight and Sergeant Dillon for three missions. The second critical substitution was for Ralph Frank,[33] aka Paddy O'Brian, the original wireless operator, who did not fly with Donald on his last two missions. He was replaced by Sergeant Ramsden and then, Sergeant Burr for the fateful Essen raid.

It is difficult to speculate about the impact of these substitutions. Some pilots were adamant that their original crew stay together, for they developed an intense loyalty and trust in each other. Donald had already fired his first navigator but appeared very confident with his replacement. Was it these changes in the crew that led to his demise? All this could be moot as the loss statistics began to pile up against bomber crews. Canadian pilot and author Murray Peden of *A Thousand Shall Fall* wrote:

> The crews faced formidable odds, odds seldom appreciated outside the Command. At times in the great offensives of 1943 and 1944, the short-term statistics foretold that less than 25 out of each 100 crews would survive their first tour of 30 operations. On a single night, Bomber Command lost more aircrew than Fighter Command lost during the Battle of Britain. Yet, the crews buckled on their chutes and set out with unshakeable resolution night after night. They fell prey to the hazards of icing, lightning, storm and structural failure, and they perished amidst the bursting shells of the flak

---

33 Frank was killed two weeks later with another crew just south of their Woodhall Spa base. The cause was unknown, but several thousand aircrew were killed in accidents and I suspect this was the cause of his death.

Chapter 12: "Regret to Inform You..."

batteries. But by far the greater number died in desperately unequal combat under the overwhelming firepower of the tenacious German night fighter defenders.[34]

On March 3, after arriving back from London, Donald wrote to his father, the words quoted at the top of this chapter. It was unusual for Donald to start a sentence with "I am afraid ..." even if it was an expression to mean "I'm sorry." Were Donald's fatalist feelings catching up to him, reminiscent of what he told his brother Bill at his departure, now that he was on dangerous missions? Did the change of crew throw Donald off, leaving him to write to his father "I have only a little while to spare?" As his teammates changed around him, Donald made the courageous decision to carry on. His March 9 letter was brief, but he was hopeful his promotion was going through. He mentioned how good the flying weather had been. As his crew left for illness and unknown reasons, did Donald sense his days were growing shorter?

Last Mission

On the night of March 12, Donald participated in the second mission to Essen. It would be his eleventh mission, his sixth in the past nine nights. On the raid to Essen that night, 97 Squadron contributed eleven aircraft to a stream of 457 bombers that attacked the key industrial centre of the German Reich. Three Lancasters of the 97 had to return due to technical failures. The principal target of the operation was the Krupp factory just west of the city centre. Donald and his crew either left the plane or crashed landed near the town of Wulfen, 25 kilometres north of Essen, suggesting that they were either on their to Essen, or on their way home when they went down.

---

34 http://www.bombercommandmuseum.ca/commandlosses.html

Night fighters and radar controlled anti-aircraft batteries provided a strong defence for Essen. As a result, 23 bombers or 5 % of the total force failed to return that night. At six to seven men in an aircraft, that would be about 150 young lives. Some would become POW's, but there was little chance of escaping to France if shot down over Germany. According to one newspaper clipping and photographic results of the raid, "12 main shops and 36 others of the Krupp works" were destroyed or damaged on that March 12th mission. The raid to Essen was an ill-fated one for the 97th Squadron; of the 11 Lancasters sent out, three returned due to mechanical failures and "One aircraft (Sgt. Plaunt) is missing."

The first people to learn of Donald's misfortune, beyond the squadron command, were a trio of airport security lads. Arthur Spencer, the author of *An Interesting War*, contributed this story to the 97 official history, *Achieve Your Aim*:

> During three months 97 Squadron lost six aircraft. One of these was Sergeant Plaunt, a Canadian, in the raid on Essen on March 12th. He lived, like most of the N.C.O.s, in a Nissen hut set in a little copse just off the road from Coningsby to Woodhall. At the end of the lane leading to the huts was a searchlight site. There were three such sites around the airfield, primarily for airfield defence, but also to form a cone over the airfield when we were returning from operations. Sergeant Plaunt had befriended and been befriended by the searchlight crew, and I remember how upset these soldiers were when he had gone missing.

Chapter 12: "Regret to Inform You..."

> REGRET TO INFORM YOU ADVICE HAS BEEN RECEIVED FROM THE ROYAL CANADIAN AIR FORCE CASUALTIES OFFICER OVERSEAS THAT DONALD CAMERON PLAUNT IS REPORTED MISSING AS THE RESULT OF AIR OPERATIONS ON MARCH THIRTEENTH NINETEEN FORTY THREE STOP IN THE BEST INTEREST OF THE POSSIBLE SAFETY OF YOUR SON IT IS REQUESTED THAT YOU WITHHOLD ANY INFORMATION FROM PRESS OR RADIO UNTIL HIS NAME APPEARS IN OFFICIAL CASUALTY LIST FIVE WEEKS HENCE STOP LETTER FOLLOWS+ RCAF CASUALTIES OFFICER

When a plane failed to return from a mission, it was the duty of the senior officer to inform both the authorities and the families of the missing crew members. Since Donald's crew consisted of three Canadians and four Brits, communication regarding the lost Canadians came initially from the RAF, with a follow-up from the RCAF to the Canadian families. After receiving the distressing telegram on Sunday, March 14, the Plaunts could only wait for news of their son's fate. There was always a faint hope that Donald would repeat Syd's escape, or that he would end up in a POW camp.

Conflicting Messages

The two Air Force commands were quick to send letters to Donald's parents with the known details of his situation. His true status would not be known until the Red Cross reported from Germany. On March 13, the 97 Squadron RAF Wing Commander, G. D. Jones, wrote the missing status letter to the Plaunts: "**Sgt Williams** (my emphasis) took part in a raid on Essen as captain of his aircraft, no news having since been received. We can but hope the aircraft was forced to land, and that the crew is safe, even as prisoners of war." Jones added that their son was "exceedingly popular, and his loss would be felt by the Squadron and his fellow men." Jones assured them that his kit would be forwarded to the RAF Central Depository for safe keeping.

For the Plaunts to read that "Sgt. Williams" was the pilot would have been most confusing. They knew that Donald was the pilot as he had emphatically told his mother in a letter of December 17, 1942, that "I am 1st pilot and captain" of the aircraft.[35] The mistake created questions, confusion and even anger.

On the 16th of March, a second letter from the Air Commodore of the RAF validated Donald's correct role as the pilot. The Air Commodore conveyed an optimistic perspective about the situation by giving the Plaunts hope that missing "does not necessarily mean that he is killed or wounded, and if he is a prisoner of war, he should be able to communicate with you." He told them that enquiries would be made through the International Red Cross to ascertain what happened to their son, and he would communicate with them any news he received. He also requested that they inform the Department of National Defence for Air in Ottawa if they received any news of their son. He added his sympathy on behalf of the Air Council and expressed his hope they would soon learn of favourable news.

A few days later, the Plaunts received their first letter from the RCAF Casualties Officer who echoed much of what the Plaunts already knew. They were told the names of the two other Canadians crew members, Pilot Officer A. J. Smith from West Summerland, B. C. and Sergeant J. L. Viau of Hull P. Q. He also told them that the "Missing in Action" would not be reported to the press for five weeks, and requested that they not speak to the media because "the publicity at this time might imperil his chance to escape." He concluded by offering them "hope that better news will be forthcoming in the near future."

---

35 This error was later corrected by the Wing Commander after my grandfather enquired why his son was not the pilot. In a letter dated May 20th he apologized for the clerical error that he confused Donald's name with Williams, the flight engineer.

Chapter 12: "Regret to Inform You..."

The 97 squadron chaplain, Hugh Davidson, hand wrote a personal note on March 23rd expressing his concern for Donald's absence. He told them he had met Donald in the crew room the day of the Essen mission. He expressed his condolences and offered his assistance if there was anything he could do. As well, an RCAF chaplain wrote a letter on March 29 offering hope and prayers for their son.

There was still one family member who needed to be told of Donald's fate, as she had not been at the family gathering on the Sunday morning when the fateful telegram arrived. Considering the news to be too delicate to telephone or telegram, the Plaunts went to Toronto to tell their youngest daughter the grim news. Jean did not know of Donald's situation as on Thursday, March 18, she recorded in her diary that she had written him a letter. The next day she received a call from her mother to tell her that she and her father were in Toronto to see her. After they told her the devastating news she spent the weekend with them and the Parkers and the Collins, family friends, formerly of Sudbury.

In the following week, Jean received a letter from her mother telling her "that it was over Essen and Williams, the co-pilot, was flying the plane." The Plaunts had not yet received the RAF Air Commodore's correction that Donald had been the pilot. In her diary, Jean recorded that she finished knitting another sweater for Donald and that her mother "is still hopeful." The following day, March 30, the principal, Miss Read, called Jean to the school office to give her a letter from Donald, postmarked March 4th. She was keeping an eye on her head girl knowing that the loss of her brother could be devastating. Jean stopped writing in her diary, but on April 17, she wrote a single sentence, "Donald's picture, etc. were in the Sudbury Star." There was no reaction in her diary to his death, although it would have been profound given their closeness.

Bill Lane wrote to Donald's mother to give his perspective on Donald's status:

> Since Don was just reported "missing," I have written the adjutant of his squadron but received no answer.

Being a mixed squadron under RAF administration and not RCAF one can hardly hope for any cooperation from them. Syd would know more of circumstances surrounding a bomber trip than I would, and he told me he thought they probably met night-fighters. It seems quite likely the crew bailed out and if such is the case, they stand a good chance of being prisoners of war. However, I don't want you to count on this too much because it's just a guess on my part. I know dozens of fellows who are listed "missing," and only a couple are prisoners. Syd is the only one I know personally that's managed to get back. I'm not trying to discourage you Mrs. Plaunt. It's just that so many people will have their ideas about what happened, and it's too easy to build one's hopes on other people's experiences.

Syd Smith would soon be able to tell the Plaunts his story as he was in London preparing to come home. While in London, he learned of Donald's death from Joe Barratt at the YMCA. There was little he could do until he got home, but the sad news prompted his memory of the last time he saw Donald at the Charing Cross Railway station. Syd remembered Donald's broad smiling face and his waving arms as he said goodbye, heading back to his squadron base. When Syd arrived in Sudbury around April 1, he immediately visited the Plaunts to try to comfort them and boost their morale with his successful escape. His story soothed their worries but not enough to bring them the news they wanted to hear.

On April 17, five weeks after Donald was shot down, his "missing status" was reported to the press. Along with another Sudbury pilot, they made the front page of *The Sudbury Star*: "600 BOMBERS CRUSH EUROPE Doucette, DFC, Don Plaunt Missing." Messages and condolences poured into the family, most notably from WB's business associates. A few could empathize with their loss as they too, had experienced the death of a son in the war.

Chapter 12: "Regret to Inform You..."

Believed to Be Killed

> REGRET TO ADVISE INTERNATIONAL RED CROSS QUOTING GERMAN INFORMATION STATES YOUR SON SERGEANT DONALD CAMERON PLAUNT LOST HIS LIFE MARCH TWELFTH STOP PENDING FURTHER CONFIRMATION YOUR SON IS TO BE CONSIDERED MISSING BELIEVED TO BE KILLED STOP PLEASE ACCEPT MY SINCERE SYMPATHY STOP LETTER FOLLOWS= RCAF CASUALTIES OFFICER

On May 9, the Plaunt's received a second telegram confirming their worst fears. Donald was "reported missing believed to be killed overseas." The "luck of the Plaunts" had run out.

In their minds, two simple questions remained to be answered: how did he die and what happened to his remains? There was much confusion over both issues as information received by the Plaunts from the RAF and the RCAF was inconsistent. For a father who was accustomed to being in control, it was most upsetting not to get a clear answer about the death of his cherished son.

The day after the Plaunts received the distressing news, Donald's mother called Syd, who was stunned at the news. And to compound the impact of Donald's death, six days later, on May 15, Bill Lane was shot down and killed in his Spitfire. Syd could only wonder why he was so lucky.

The RCAF Casualties officer followed up with a letter on May 15th with more details from the International Red Cross. "Your son lost his life on March 12, 1943, and was buried in the Cemetery at Wulfen." The report also stated that the two other Canadians, Pilot Officer Smith and Sergeant Viau, are buried in the same cemetery as your son. There was no mention of the four British crew members as the RAF had dealt with them.

Frustrated with the incorrect information in the first letter from Donald's Wing Commander, WB began to enquire through his connections. He contacted his cousin, FX Plaunt, of Montreal, whose nephew, Frank Wait, was posted at the RCAF headquarters in London. On May 6, Wait responded to his uncle that news had been received by the Red Cross that Donald was the captain of the Lancaster, but that only two of the three Canadian crew had been identified and buried. There was no information on Donald, nor of the four RAF crew members. Wait concluded: "From the information we have, it is most difficult to say what happened. The two chaps that were found may have bailed out and were killed on landing, or they may have been the only two identifiable after a crash. On the other hand, they may have been the only two who died in the crash, and the rest of the crew may have escaped or have been taken prisoner."

One can only imagine the confusion and anxiety that Wait's letter created for Donald's parents. It would have arrived well after the May 9 telegram that reported that Donald was "presumed killed" and now, according to Wait, there was no identified body of their son. Given the contradiction between the two letters, how could they find out what happened?

Donald's neighbourhood friends were most upset when they learned of his death. Jim Hinds remembered that after Donald was reported killed, Andy Grieve, his grade eight teacher, pointed to the seat that Donald sat in, and told the class of the sad news. The first student through the doors of Alexander was now the school's first casualty of war.

Donald's mother was remarkably accepting of Donald's death and on May 11 she wrote her mother and sister Pearl of the heartbreaking news.

> This will just be a short note, with not very happy news. We had a wire from Ottawa on Sunday evening saying that Donald had lost his life on the night of March 12, so reports the German Red Cross.

Chapter 12: "Regret to Inform You..."

So that's final.

I never did have much hope, if any, that he would have landed safely. The area is too well fortified and Essen is one of their best manufacturing cities. That's all the news we got, so if he died that night, he didn't suffer long. I called Miss Read last evening and talked to Jean this morning.

Don't feel too badly. He lived a full happy life and perhaps accomplished more in his almost 21 years of living than some people do in a lifetime, and if he, and other lads before him, were not ready to go and die, where would we all be? He chose to do this and he did it in his own way.

We could have done lots of things to dissuade him from his training but he would have none of it. He was getting what he got on his own, and he got what he wanted, which was to be a pilot on a Lancaster bomber. He was one of the first Canadians to fly a Lancaster.

Must stop now.

WB and I went up to Wye Saturday and home Sunday. Awful Lonesome. I would see Donald tearing up the path and shouting "Where do we eat?"

Love to all,

Mildred

The RCAF Casualties Officer wrote one final letter (June 29) confirming Donald's death and the location where he was buried. A report had been received: "quoting official German information, which states, that your son, Sergeant Donald Cameron Plaunt, was buried on March 17th, in the Municipal Cemetery, Section 2 Wulfen. As this is official German information, Presumption of Death action is being instituted by the Air Ministry and when your son's death has been officially presumed, you will be advised by telegram." A further telegram (no date) confirmed his death on March 12 along with, "Please accept my deepest sympathies."

Missing Remains

Although Donald's mother accepted his death, the seeds of doubt continued to fester within his father concerning the circumstances surrounding Donald's death. Soon after the war was over in Europe, he asked Al Flood, a good friend of his daughter Helen and a corporal in the RCAF, to visit the Wulfen cemetery to verify what the RCAF had told the Plaunts regarding the burial of Donald. On August 7, Flood wrote more disturbing news:

Flood's photo of Wulfen cemetery: from L to R, markers for Viau, Williams, Dillon and Smith

At my first view of the cemetery I was greatly put out at its condition but was soon put on the right track when I contacted the British Army unit in Wulfen. A good part of the cemetery had been bombed and suffered three or four direct hits. The cemetery is not big by any means, so you can readily imagine the damage. I looked high and low for Donald's grave but failed.

Before I go much further, I had better tell you the kind of day it was. It doesn't take a great deal of explaining except that it was raining, and raining hard. The English soldier that came to the cemetery with me took me to the graves of some soldiers and airmen that had recently been transferred and buried in the cemetery, but none was Donald's. The pictures you will receive are of the graves, but the names on the crosses are not very legible as it was a very poor day for taking pictures.

Flood also related what he had heard concerning the Commonwealth dead who were buried in various German cemeteries. The Graves Commission would identify each man's grave and remark it. In a few years, all these graves would be transferred to one of four cemeteries to be looked after by the Commonwealth Graves Commission. He told them that every next of kin would be advised where their loved one is buried. Flood expressed his sympathy and promised to check the Wulfen cemetery if he happened to be in the area in the future.

WB's reaction at receiving Flood's news was swift. He contacted the RCAF Casualties Officer for an explanation. The officer responded that bombs had destroyed Donald's grave, but assured him that his body was in the cemetery. Flood's letter only confirmed in WB's mind that something was amiss.

The suspicions surrounding Donald's missing body raised a general question regarding what happened to the seven crew members that night. A story circulated among our family after the war that something untoward happened to the crew after they bailed out of their plane the night of March 12. Apparently, Dr. Bill White, a Sudbury doctor in the Canadian Army, had told our family a very different story from the one the Air Force had communicated to the Plaunts. According to White's story, the airplane had been shot down, and the seven crew members had safely parachuted to the ground. They were rounded up and executed by a firing squad, which was a common fate of some aircrews who landed in Germany. What was unknown to me was the reason why Dr. White was in Wulfen. There were two possibilities. He may have been investigating the crew's death as a war crime, since shooting captured airmen is a violation of the Geneva Convention. The Convention requires that warring countries are to take captured military prisoners to POW camps and notify the prisoners' government, usually through the Red Cross. In Germany, these rules were followed if the army or civilian police captured the Allied aircrew. However, it was speculated that Donald's crew was picked up by one of two groups that were known to murder their captives: civilians who resented the bombing of their homes, or the SS, who never followed any laws and simply shot them upon capture. Donald and his crew were reportedly executed and buried at Wulfen.

When I began researching Donald's biography years ago, I asked Alan Thepheads, a London volunteer I made through a Bomber Command website, to see if there was any truth to this story. He had found that there had been a War Crimes case against the SS for three Allied airmen, but that was in Essen, and there was nothing in Wulfen that he could find. Alan spent countless hours in the Public Records Office researching my uncle's missions and sent the research to me. Unfortunately, I didn't know where to take this further to confirm or deny the crew execution story, and I stopped pursuing it.

In retrospect, I have my doubts about the War Crimes investigation viewpoint. Until recently, I did not know about Al Flood's letter and his photograph, nor the explanation for the missing grave. I have the photo he took, but didn't realize that Donald's marker was missing because the names were initially unreadable. When the names became clearer with photo editing, Donald's marker was still not present. It is possible the

Chapter 12: "Regret to Inform You..."

graves were bombed after the German submitted their report, and the explosions may well have destroyed Donald's grave since Flood could not find it.

There is the second possibility to explain White's presence in the Wulfen cemetery. I now wonder if Donald's father had asked him to check to see if Donald's grave had been found. Unfortunately, I never had the opportunity to discuss this with Dr. White. However, since Donald and his crew were reported missing, there is a possibility we will learn what happened to them. The Missing Research and Enquiry Service was involved in Donald's case, and they might have investigated the discrepancy between the official military report and the letters my grandfather had received from Wait and Flood. To find that report might clarify the mix-up. I learned recently that the Casualty Reports are in the process of being made public (on-line), but it will indubitably take some time as they are beginning in 1939 and are releasing reports in chronological order.[36] Although it may take a few years, I will post the report on my website (pogamasing.com) when it is released.

The week before the war ended, Donald's father wrote to the Chief of Air Staff that he had heard of the possibility of moving the remains of boys killed in Germany to another country. If this was the case, he wanted to know the name of the person he could contact to learn more about returning Donald's remains to Canada. An RCAF officer replied that removal to Canada, or any other country, was not permissible under the present policy of the Canadian Armed Forces. In due time, all Canadian military dead were to be eventually located in an Imperial War Graves Cemetery in Germany. After receiving Flood's report and photos, Plaunt wrote the Air Force Chief of Staff that his son's grave could not be found where he was told it was buried. Now that the war was over, Plaunt was hoping for a change of policy and would like to know if it was being

---

36 RAF website where these reports will be released: http://www.rafcommands.com/tags/casualty-packs/ As of Sept. 16, 2016, reports have been issued up to August 16, 1940.

considered. The Air Staff's response assured him that the "Imperial War Graves Commission will do everything humanly possible to ascertain the exact location of your son's grave." A further letter explained that the War Graves Commission had explored the possibility of returning bodies to their respective countries but disallowed it because "to allow the removal of a few personnel would be contrary to the principle of equality of treatment."

Final Resting

Temporary marker in Reichswald Forest War Cemetery taken by Mildred or WB Plaunt

In a letter to the Plaunts dated January 21, 1949, the RCAF Casualties Officer wrote that "the graves of your son and six other members of his crew[37] have been moved to the permanent British (later Commonwealth)

---

37   The six other crew members were: T. L Williams, A. J. Smith, J-L Viau, W. C. Burr, A. W. Taylor, G. W. Dillon

Chapter 12: "Regret to Inform You..."

Military Cemetery in the Reichswald Forest, Germany." He gave the location. "Your son is resting in grave # 4 Row B, Plot 17, of the cemetery and the numbers of his crew are resting beside him in graves 1, 2, 3, 5, 6, and 7." One year later, Donald's parents visited his grave with their close friends, George and Dorothy Miller, and took photographs of the white cross of their son's temporary marker.

Shortly after their visit, the Imperial War Graves Commission sent a letter to Donald's parents illustrating a diagram of the permanent headstone "that would mark each grave; thus every man, rich or poor, General or Private, will be honoured in the same way." They were also asked to contribute a personal inscription for the headstone. The Plaunts paraphrased a line from Henry Longfellow's poem, *Resignation*: "IN THAT GREAT CLOISTER'S STILLNESS HE LIVES WHOM WE CALL DEAD." [38]

Final Markers for Donald and his Crew in The Reichswald Forest War Cemetery: W. Burr, G. Dillon, D. C. Plaunt, A. J. Smith, A. W. Taylor, J.-L. Viau, T. L. Williams

---

38 See: http://www.hwlongfellow.org/poems_poem.php?pid=117

Aftermath

Despite his anger over Donald's death and the subsequent uncertainty around the circumstances, his father reluctantly acknowledged his son's fate. One poignant story that illustrated his acceptance came from Jean's best friend, Sheila O'Reilly. Although Sheila did not know that the Plaunts had sent monthly boxes of Laura Secord chocolates to Donald, she witnessed the heartbreaking conclusion.

Once Donald arrived in England, he realized there were many things he could not buy that he enjoyed in Canada. One of his favourite treats was Laura Secord chocolates. Consequently, he asked his father if he would send him a box. Donald's appreciative comments in his letters brought more 'Lauras' from other members of the family. Soon after, WB put in a standing order with the local Laura Secord store to send Donald a box every month.

One day after school in early May of 1943, Sheila was in the Laura Secord store. She was surprised to see Mr. Plaunt enter as it was not the kind of place she would expect to meet him. Donald's death had been announced, and she was aware of its impact on the family as she had been in touch with Jean. Noticing Sheila, WB came over and after a short chat, excused himself. He approached the clerk and asked to settle his account. Sheila told Jean about seeing her father and then learned from her why he was in the candy store that day.

A few months later, the young clerk who served WB that day, told Jean that the saddest day of her life was that day her father came into the store. At first, the clerk assumed he came to pay his account. Sadly, it was to cancel the monthly order.

I have related the details of Donald's death and the subsequent issues raised by his father to sort out the confusion which created additional distress over Donald's loss. However, there was a consoling side to his death. Friends, business associates, and former teachers swamped the Plaunts with letters and visits. As well, public figures, such as the King and Queen, Chubby Powers, the Minister of National Defence and George Drew, the

Premier of Ontario, sent letters of condolences. In various statements, they expressed their "heartfelt sympathy in your sorrow" to "the gratitude of government for the life of a brave man freely given in the service of his country." On January 12, 1944, Donald's mother received a Memorial Cross, better known as the "Silver Cross" from John McNab, Group Captain, Command Chaplain "as a token of the sacrifice which you have made for our cause through the passing of your son."

If the letters my grandparents received, both officially from Ottawa, and from their friends and business associates was an indication of the depth of sympathy every time a Canadian died, it was a remarkable testament to the appreciation of the Canadian people for the sacrifice so many young men made. The letters were a recognition that the parents had lost something irreplaceable as well.

As Donald had mentioned in a letter to his father, he had discussions with his Wing Commander regarding his promotion. According to his military file, he was promoted on January 16, 1943, shortly after his first interview. However, he would have been very disappointed as it was to the lesser rank of Warrant Officer Class II, rather than to a real commission of Pilot Officer, which Syd and Bill had received, and Donald had expected.

The memory of Donald's name has been carried on in the family. In an earlier letter to his brother Bill, Donald listed the possible names for Bill and Agnes' expected son. There was no doubt what it would be now, and Donald Cameron Plaunt was born on June 23, 1943. As well, in 1945, my mother demonstrated her affection for her brother by naming her third child, Judith Cameron Plaunt Thomson. She wanted to include "Donald" but was overruled by her father as there already was one.

Syd Smith, the only survivor of the Musketeers, did not forget his friends and named two of his sons, Donald Cameron Smith and William Thompson Smith (after Bill Lane).

CHAPTER 13

The Uncle I Came to Know

"It would be difficult to conceive of anyone who could do more for the morale of a crew than Donald Plaunt." Acta Ridleianna

My Uncle Donald was a statistic, one of over 18,000 Canadian airmen who died while flying for the RCAF in the Second World War. More importantly, he was the son, brother and uncle of a family. The statistic conveys the extent of the sacrifice the country made for Canada's participation in the air war. The monetary cost[39] cannot compare to the loss of these young men to so many families.

Impact on Donald's Family

The pain that parents experience after the death of a child is unknowable to those who have not suffered it. By custom, it is assumed that it is the mother who is most devastated. For the loss, the government presents her with a silver cross. The father, on the other hand, is expected to show a stiff upper lip and get over it. However, according to Donald's brother Bill, his father was deeply impacted by his younger son's death. "His death

---

[39] According to http://www.canadaatwar.ca/content-7/world-war-ii/facts-and-information/ the war cost Canada over $21 Billion

Chapter 13: The Uncle I Came to Know

took the heart out of him," he told me. By that, he meant his life didn't seem as purposeful after Donald's death. His father loved and treated all his children equally, and he was generous with each one of them, but he had a very special relationship with his younger son. For my grandfather's generation, boys were highly valued, and along with his closeness to his younger son as a result of spending more time him growing up, his death was heartbreaking.

I have no written account of my grandfather's reaction to Donald's death. He was a very private man and didn't share his innermost feelings, even with his family. However, I believe he would have been angry about the misinformation he received from Donald's Wing Commander and the confusion regarding his burial. I imagine he eventually came to terms with Donald's death in his way and accepted the fact, that if his son was gone, he wanted his community to know the great sacrifice Donald and his family had made. He did this by contributing to several memorials in Donald's honour including an operating room at the Sudbury Memorial Hospital, and the building fund for a Memorial Hall at Ridley for all the Second World War dead. As well, he arranged for several plaques in his honour (see Appendix B) and he framed many military photographs of his son.

Donald's mother was deeply stung, but she appeared to accept his death more calmly. Perhaps her closeness to her four daughters and her numerous grandchildren helped to disperse her pain. It is worth repeating what she wrote to her mother after receiving the news of his death:

> Don't feel too badly. He lived a full happy life and perhaps accomplished more in his almost 21 years of living than some people do in a lifetime, and if he and other lads before him were not ready to go and die where would we all be? He chose to do this, and he did it in his own way.

There would always be poignant memories of him. In the same letter, Donald's mother wrote: "WB and I went up to Wye Saturday and home Sunday. Awful Lonesome. I would see Donald tearing up the path and shouting; "Where do we eat?" His presence would continue to be felt in all those places and experiences which Donald shared with his family. As well, his parents kept all the letters, telegrams, and photographs Donald had sent them. These mementos were a way of keeping his memory alive, much like the intent of Longfellow's verse they chose for their son's marker.

While reading through my manuscript about Donald's leave in Devon, I was struck by another example of my Nana's yearning to stay connected to him. I recalled that her favourite perfume was called *Devon Violets*. For me, this scent evoked her presence, as much as her warm smile and gentle voice. And I wondered - was there a connection between this perfume and Donald's many gifts to her? To check my hunch, I emailed my sister Judy with the question. She responded: "OMG, YES!!! Uncle Donald used to buy her that perfume, and she never wore anything else for the rest of her life. I have one of her old bottles, and once in awhile I smell the lid, and it reminds me of Nana and Uncle Donald."

To Donald's siblings, he would forever be their baby brother, their carefree Buggs who they loved deeply. Their memories of his boundless enthusiasm and cheerfulness would be his legacy. They too kept their mementos, photos, letters and the memory of their fallen brother. Donald's brother Bill donated a trophy - The Donald Plaunt Memorial Trophy - to the Northern Ontario Football League for the league championship. Every Plaunt household had his photograph in a prominent place in their homes. My mother kept a cameo photo of Donald on her bedroom dresser.

Chapter 13: The Uncle I Came to Know

Loss to His Friends

Beyond his family, there was the impact on his closest buddies, Syd and Bill. The three boyhood friends had dreamed of enlisting together. They had hoped to train together, but only Donald and Syd were called up at the same time. Once overseas, the "Musketeers" kept in touch through letters, visits and leaves in London. Syd was the only one who survived the war, and as noted earlier, he named two of his sons in their honour. Syd's summation of Donald's character was an astute description of his carefree spirit: "I took vicarious delight in the spontaneous pranks of Don, the charmer, the rule-breaker, the irrepressible teenager living life to the deepest and fullest, plunging into deep water wherever he went." Of Syd's original "Brotherhood of Thirteen," the 13 boys from Sudbury High who joined the Air Force, only four came home. The Lanes lost two of their five sons in the war, and a third son resented being held back from going overseas and suffered a self-destructive demise through alcohol.

Joseph Barratt, the YMCA director in Sudbury, and later in London during the war, wrote a heartfelt letter to the Plaunts:

> While I have been overseas, I have come to know Donnie along with his pals, Bill Lane and Sydney Smith, and they were three great pals. Just three weeks ago tomorrow, Bill Lane and I were talking over the telephone, and he told me he had received word definitely, that your dear son, Donnie was declared "killed in action." Naturally, it was a terrible blow to me, as I had seen him not long before he left on his last trip. Sydney Smith will likely have told you of the exploits of the three pals overseas, and of his escape too. We all hoped that Don would be lucky too, but the worst has happened. Now, his other pal, Bill Lane is missing, and we do not hold out much hope for him.

I write this wee note to assure you of my sincere sympathy in the terrible loss you have suffered, but I would like to assure you, that Don did a grand job over here, he was loyal and liked his work. He loved his pals, and they were true chums together, in a mission of which we all know. On every occasion I had to meet Don, I can assure you he always thought of the folks back home, and naturally, as he loved his home and all that it means to youth, and most of all he loved his two parents.

His School Remembers

Donald's death had a profound impact on his Ridley friends and teachers. John Sale, a classmate of Donald's, remembered that Porky was one of the first Ridleians to die whom the boys at the school knew. His death brought a poignant reminder of the grim reality of war. There were fine tributes to their admired Porky in *Acta Ridleianna*, and in letters from his Ridley teachers to the Plaunts. He had spent his formative years there and had developed a special relationship with the school. An obituary in the *Acta* (Midsummer '43) was a meaningful tribute to one of their own:

> Seldom has the School been so shocked and filled with a feeling of personal loss, as many of the boys still at the School remember "Porky's" familiar figure on the campus. Don came to Ridley from Sudbury in September 1937, a total stranger to everyone, but it was not long before his cheerful disposition and happy smile had won him a host of friends. He quickly absorbed the spirit of Ridley and early in his school career displayed qualities of leadership, which steadily developed during his four years at the school. He took an active part in all School activities. It would be difficult to conceive of anyone

Chapter 13: The Uncle I Came to Know

who could do more for the morale of a crew than Donald Plaunt. In his heroic death, Ridley has lost a fine Old Boy, one who had he lived, was destined to make his mark in some line of endeavour. If he had to go, we know that he would not have chosen any other way than that of doing his duty to his country and his School.

The headmaster, Dr. Griffith, wrote to the Plaunts:

> It was with a feeling of deepest sorrow and personal loss that I read your letter telling me of Donald's death.
>
> My heart goes out to you and Mrs. Plaunt for I know how deep your grief must be. Donald was always a most interesting boy to me while he was at Ridley because I always felt that he had in him the qualities of real manhood. He was a sportsman in the truest sense of the term, and he proved this by his early desire to do his share in defence of all that is worthwhile in this world.
>
> I know that words seem so empty at such a time as this, but I do want you and Mrs. Plaunt to know that as long as Ridley lasts, Donald's name and memory will live in the school. He was a most loyal son of Ridley, and I feel a great personal loss in his passing.

Donald's mother received a most touching request from his Ridley housemaster and teacher, J. R. Hamilton.

> As you well know, I was sincerely fond of Donald, and his name is often mentioned between Mr. Matheson and me. There are so many incidents, some of them trifling, which stand out in my memory of Donald's life at Ridley.

Write Soon and Often

First of all – his infectious smile, his pride in his plaid dressing gown, which he and I purchased here, his love of hockey, and his unique sense of humour. I would like so much to have a photograph of him. I hesitate to say this as I feel sure you have so many friends and relatives who would naturally wish one. I can assure you that he is well remembered by all those at Ridley who knew him.

In the Ridley history, *The Story of the School*, author Kim Beattie described Donald as "the cheery Porky" and along with another fighter pilot, Les Ashburner, "were the kind of boys who had left Ridley, something of themselves and who would be remembered forever by their Ridley generation." The school honoured the Ridley boys who gave their lives in the Second World War by constructing a white marble wall as a memorial to the 80 Ridleians who lost their lives. Their deaths were the tip of the iceberg of the number of Ridleians who served in the war. With an annual enrollment of under 300 students in the Senior School, approximately 1,200 of them served in the Second World War. They lived their school motto "Terar Dum Posim": May I be consumed in service.

Memorial Plaque in the Ridley College Chapel

Coming of Age

Donald's time in the Air Force bridged that seminal passage from adolescence to adulthood. He moved from an advantaged family and school life into the midst of a war that forced him to face challenges beyond his

Chapter 13: The Uncle I Came to Know

control. In that transition, Donald experienced an accelerated coming of age, similar to all young men thrust into war.

Donald was a unique character. He was a very privileged kid who lacked for little, even during the Depression. How many kids back then had a car, a private school education, a trip to Europe and most importantly, a family who adored him? I must admit there were times when I read his orders to his mother for Air Force shirts, black Oxfords and copious groceries, especially Lauras, I thought he was a bit overindulged. Despite this self-centeredness, his indulgences were eclipsed by his concern and generosity towards others: his request to his mother to send clothes for a Sudbury recruit who had little; his plan to protect his Jewish comrade; his request for a Christmas basket for his rear gunner's three-year-old daughter and cigarettes for his crew. Even the evolution of his refrain of "Write soon and often" to "I'll write as soon as I can" reflected a growth in his maturity.

As we have seen through his letters, Donald grew up in a number of ways. Once he became a pilot of the Lancaster, he became the skipper of a crew of six other men, and their lives depended on his capability to fly safely every time they took off. And it wasn't just those six lives: as the youngest member of his crew, he also had the wives and children of his crew to worry about. That alone carried a heavy responsibility. Then he led his crew from the training airfields of Britain to the treacherous skies over Germany filled with anti-aircraft guns and night fighters. All the privileges in the world could not help him survive this war; it was primarily competence, but mostly good luck.

He learned that people of different ethnic groups did not fit his preconceptions. At Kinloss, he met two crew members who challenged his stereotypes of French Canadians and Jews. He was soon boasting about what a crazy bunch they all were and how much he enjoyed them. He was prepared to shield the identity of his Jewish wireless operator by altering his name to Paddy O'Brian, or by exchanging his identity tag with him when flying on missions. He described his crew as "the great melting pot," given the variety of ethnic groups in his crew. His self-revelation of "once you get to know them" became an important one in dispelling the stereotypes he once held.

He also had strong views about many issues of the day that changed little over this period, such as his criticism of some French Canadians who, in his mind, shirked their duty, and his disrespect for the Canadian prime minister. He became a Canadian nationalist, both from his European travels in 1939 and possibly from his dislike of many things British: the women who stuck their noses up at Canadians, the conflict between labour and capital, and his antipathy towards the RAF brass, especially over their promotion policy. He had much praise for his British crew members and certainly what he called "the world's best bomber," the Lancaster he flew.

Although he never mentioned it in his letters, there was a trait that I admired in my uncle and in all who served our country - their courage. Many enlisted because it was the thing to do, or for the adventure. What could be more daring and fun than to fly a fighter plane and be a hero? Donald's response to his reason for enlisting was "It's the proper thing to do." However, once these young recruits were in the service and began to train, they learned of the real consequences. To get in that airplane every day, knowing that some pilots and aircrew on each mission would not return, took a lot of guts. Many couldn't take it, but Donald stayed with it, as did thousands of others.

Donald and many other young men gave the ultimate gift while serving their country. In the fateful roll of the dice, with a 50/50 chance, he came out on the wrong side. Young men rarely consider this possibility when they enlist; their bravado outweighs the thought of losing their lives. I mentioned the possibility that Donald told his brother at the railway station that he didn't think he'd return. However, his letters contradicted that story, as he always said he was looking forward to coming back, attending a university with his sister after his tour of duty, and buying a flashy Cadillac convertible. But then, looking to the future was the only way to deal with the dreadful and uncertain circumstances these airmen found themselves in.

Chapter 13: The Uncle I Came to Know

The Importance of Letters

Donald and his friends were so eager to enlist in the Air Force. I wonder if they ever considered what their lives would be like once they were overseas. He expressed much enthusiasm and confidence during the Canadian phase of his training. But at that point, contact with family and friends was easily attained. For Donald, he could visit his family in Sudbury or southern Ontario. Once overseas, his friendships had to eclipse his family support. He was constantly in touch, either by letter, phone or visits, with his friends from Ridley, Sudbury and with those he had met during his training. He was a very social fellow who valued his friendships. He enjoyed his crew and wrote enthusiastically about the enjoyment they shared in their Nissen hut. But once he crossed the Atlantic letters were the only way to communicate with his family. They became the life line for his morale.

Although I started this project with a focus on my uncle, I was struck by the role his family played in supporting Donald: primarily it was through their letters and boxes of food and gifts. But there were subtle impacts as well, such as the satisfaction he got when he took a brief look at his "rogues gallery" of family photos in a small picture wallet he carried with him. He demonstrated a genuine interest in his "band of tigers." He craved frequent contact, suggesting a strong desire to be in touch with the people he loved. He missed them and even admitted to being homesick to his sisters Jean and Helen. His prolific letter-writing always came with the expectation of a speedy reply. Donald had a need to both hear from his family, and at the same time, to inform them that he was still alive, although his frequent telegrams did that more promptly.

Could Donald, or all the soldiers, sailors, and airmen, have performed as well without this support? Often families were unable to contact each other during periods of the war. Air Force men were usually stationed in a safe location and could get mail and boxes from home easier than the Navy or Army personnel once they were in combat zones. The military knew the importance of family contact and made a concerted attempt to support this communication.

There was another purpose to his letter writing. For him, it was a common antidote for the anxiety he experienced during the war. His comrades dealt with the stress by going out to pubs and having a few beers. This activity was not something Donald wanted to do, not just to keep his commitment to his father, but because he was troubled by those who could not hold their liquor. He found a different way to deal with the stress in a way that suited him - writing letters in his Nissen hut by a coal-fired stove, wolfing down a few Lauras. It wasn't that he was anti-social, as he was clearly a very gregarious person. It was clear that this regular communication by mail maintained his emotional balance. The stress that he developed during the day could be deflated by reading letters from his family and writing to them at night.

Donald's letters home varied in tone and content according to whom he was writing. His mother was his touchstone. She provided the widest range of purposes, often being his confessor in whom he unloaded some of his deepest sentiments, his beliefs about fate or his frustrations, especially at not receiving letters. At times, he was demanding, expecting her to write more letters, order his clothes and food supplies, or buy presents for the family. To his father, Donald was more controlled, teasing him for being modest about his golfing victories, and discussing politics, business and the war. He also knew how to "make a touch" with a man who loved him so much he could not refuse his requests. His father's fear of losing him created a need to give his son anything he wanted, just in case it was the last time he had the opportunity. But as Donald wrote to Jean, his parents "are the only two that matter." He loved them deeply.

To his youngest and closest sister Jean, he played the clown and the know-it-all big brother. He teased her about her boyfriends, cajoled her into following his advice on what he thought was best for her and called her all the flashiest and sexist terms teenagers used in that era. His letters to Jean generated the most vivid language and humour of all his letters. Despite his mild teasing, underneath he demonstrated a deep caring and

Chapter 13: The Uncle I Came to Know

generosity towards her. He could tell Jean things that he couldn't say to his parents, as he did not want to alarm them about what was happening to many of his friends. With his older siblings, he was calmer yet witty, interested in their children and their lives, sharing news, and expressing his appreciation of their letters and boxes of treats.

I suspect that most servicemen did not get the abundant mail and bountiful packages that Donald received. There were times when I was surprised by the mail orders he requested from his mother. However, as he matured, the outbursts subsided, and his regular expression of appreciation surpassed his requests.

I found sources for my uncle's life in many different mediums: photos and personal recollections from family, friends and teachers; military records; internet sites and books. However, for me, the heart of his story came from his letters, for they conveyed who he was: his personality, thoughts, values, concerns and sense of humour. It was through Donald's letters I truly came to know him.

Donald's letters candidly portrayed his love of family and friends, his generosity and his commitment to duty. They also display his remarkable and amusing wit. The notes home also revealed the maturing in Donald's character where we witnessed a broader spectrum of his humanity. Over the course of his letter-writing, we noticed a change from his self-centredness and entitlement to his thoughtfulness and appreciation; from his narrow perspective to his openness; from his expectation of becoming an officer, to living happily with a crew of sergeants; and from his vulnerability to his beaming self-confidence. In a nutshell, we followed his development from an entitled rookie pilot to the proud captain of a Lancaster crew. Although he became disillusioned with some aspects of the RAF and talked of returning to Canada, he remained committed to performing his duty. As mentioned above, his letter endings in the last couple of months of his life encapsulated his growth: from "Write soon and often" to "I'll write again soon."

My Appointment

So what drew me to my uncle's story? I believe I was first fated to write my uncle's biography the day I saw his name "waiting for me" in a Second World War *Book of Remembrance* in the Peace Tower. I recently learned, however, that someone had selected me much earlier. Ironically, it came from the photograph that sat on my parent's mantle the entire time I was a kid until my mother sold her home in 1996. A few months ago, and long after I was engaged in this book, I glanced at my bookshelf and noticed the metallic-framed photo stuffed in between family memorabilia. I wondered, "Perhaps there was information on the back of the picture that would answer my question regarding its origins." So I pulled it out and withdrew the photograph from the frame. What I found overwhelmed me. On the back of my uncle's photo was a hand-written note to me from my grandmother: "To Andrew on your third birthday, 1944." My wife Mandy's response, "She recruited you back then to tell his story!"

And there was more. Scotch-taped on the underside of the photograph was a poem, "This Was My Brother," hand-written by me in grade seven. I searched and found its author - Mona Gould - who had written about her brother who died at Dieppe. Her sentiments echoed my feelings about my uncle, but I had no recollection of having done this school project over 60 years ago. Fortunately, my mother had placed it with Uncle Donald's picture, hoping I would find it one day. If only she knew how her action helped me to re-connect with her beloved brother. The photo now sits in a more prominent place on my desk.

Unforgettable Stories

There are a couple of other poignant stories of Donald's legacy worth mentioning. One came from the unintended consequence of my uncle's generosity. When Donald gave his box of Lauras to his rear gunner Jock's three-year-old daughter and asked his mother to send her a Christmas

Chapter 13: The Uncle I Came to Know

box, he began a tradition that extended long after both of their deaths. Jock lived on a disability pension for the rest of his life, although he stayed in touch with Donald's family. The former rear gunner developed his artistic skills and often sent his artwork to my grandparents, including a painted portrait of his former captain. Donald's mother continued to send boxes and money to them both at Christmas and Easter. After my grandmother's death, my mother continued the annual gifts until Jock's death, and after that to Margaret, his second wife. Then my sister Kathie kept the contact with Margaret and was still in touch by telephone, until her death this January.

I have saved the most unbelievable story for the ending. It is so poignant and astonishing that I sometimes have difficulty telling it. It shatters the concept of six degrees of separation. I heard the story from Jean, the sister he loved to tease and cajole, but whom he dearly loved as he proudly wore her pin on his battledress. The incident occurred in her Florida retirement community where there were other Canadians. Every week for many years, the same group of women would get together to play bridge. On one occasion, one of these women asked Jean's permission to use her telephone. When she returned to the table, she told Jean that she noticed her name on an envelope, written as Jean "Plaunt" Benness. Her guest had known her only as Jean Benness and was curious about her middle name. Jean replied that Plaunt was her maiden name.

The woman then told her this incredible story: "When I was a young girl I lived in Holland and attended school in Nijmegen before my family immigrated to Canada. There were special days every year when my school took us to the Reichswald War Cemetery just over the border in Germany. It contained the graves of over 7,500 Commonwealth soldiers and airmen, of which there were just over 700 Canadian airmen. We did some gardening to keep the grounds looking beautiful since we Dutch are grateful to the Canadians who liberated us, and gave their lives in doing so. As well as doing some general gardening, each student was assigned to look after one grave. The grave that I looked after belonged to a pilot by the name of Donald Plaunt!" These two women had played bridge together for years and didn't realize they shared this unbelievable link.

This story began as a personal connection to my uncle because of a picture that got my attention when I was thirteen years old. It was a black and white photograph that sat on our mantle with a poem in the back I had used to commemorate him for a school project in grade seven. Mona Gould had written the poem about the brother she lost at Dieppe. The words she chose and the feelings that radiated from her lines, attracted me as if I had written the poem myself. 73 years after he was killed I still feel a deep connection towards my uncle and his story. And now, I can finally put to rest my questions and wonderings about who he was as a friend, as a brother, as a son, and as an uncle.

Chapter 13: The Uncle I Came to Know

This was my brother
At Dieppe,
Quietly a hero
Who gave his life
Like a gift,
Withholding nothing.

His Youth ... his love ...
His enjoyment of being alive ...
His future, like a book
With half the pages still uncut.

APPENDIX A
Chronology of Donald Plaunt's Life

EVENTS	DATE	LOCATION
Early Life		
Birth	June 1, 1922	North Bay
Elementary School	Sept. 1928/30, 1930/36	Central Public, Alexander
Secondary School	Sept. 1936/37	Subury High School
	Sept. 37/May 41	Ridley College
Trip to Europe	July/August 1939	UK, Belgium, France, Germany
Enlistment and Training		
Recruitment	April 8, 1941	North Bay
Enlistment	May 23	Hamilton
Manning Depot	May 23	Toronto
Guard Duty	June 21	St. Thomas
Initial Training School	July 27	Toronto

Appendix A: Chronology of Donald Plaunt's Life

Elementary Flying School	Sept. 2	Goderich
Service Flying Training School	Oct. 26	Brantford
Disembarkment from Halifax	March 23, 1942	Halifax

Overseas Training

Arrival UK	Mar. 25 – end of April	Bournemouth
Blind Approach Training	May 1 - 25, 1942	Dishforth **RAF** 26, 27
Advanced Flying Unit #6	June 25 - July 22	Little Rissington
New posting	July 22 - 29	Topcliffe. **RAF** 40
Operational Training Unit [#19]	Aug. 11 - Oct. 21	Kinloss, Scotland, **RAF** 43
Heavy Conversion Unit [1660]	Oct. 27 - Dec. 15	Swinderby, **RAF** 19-84

Operations

Squadron 97	Dec. 15 Feb. 24 to Mar 2	Woodhall Spa leave, met with Syd, Bill
Essen, 11th mission	Mar. 12/13	shot down over Wulfen

207

Aftermath

Promotion	Jan. 15, 1943	W.O., II Class, posthumous
Reported Missing	Mar. 15	
Reported Killed, Buried	May, 1943	Wulfen, 30 k's north of Essen
Final Burial	1949	Reichswald Forest War Cemetery, Germany

APPENDIX B

List of Memorials Where Donald Plaunt's Name is Listed

1. **Peace Tower, Parliament Building,** Ottawa (http://www.veterans.gc.ca/eng/remembrance/memorials/books)

2. **Bomber Command Museum,** Nanton, Alberta (http://www.bombercommandmuseum.ca/index.html)

3. **British Commonwealth Air Training Museum,** Brandon Manitoba (not seen) memorial wall with 19,286 names of air crew who died during WW II (http://www.airmuseum.ca/memorial/)

4. **York Minister Cathedral,** York, England. RAF memorial to 18,000 aircrew who gave their lives in WW II who were based in Yorkshire, Northumberland and Durham

5. **They Shall Not Grow Old**: A Book of Remembrance of over 18,000 Canadian aircrew who were enlisted in the RCAF and lost their lives in WW II.

6. **Memorial Park,** Sudbury (https://www.cdli.ca/monuments/on/sudbury2.htm)

7. **Knox Presbyterian Church,** Sudbury

8. **Sudbury High School**

9. **Ridley College** WW II Memorial Wall, St. Catharines, ON

Other Memorials

1. Plaques - Ridley College Memorial Chapel, St. Catharines

    Plaunt Family Memorial, Lake Pogamasing,

    Memorial Hospital, Sudbury

2. Trophy - **Donald Plaunt Memorial Trophy** for the championship of the Northern Football Conference donated by his brother Bill Plaunt